W9-AWG-663

THE INSTANT TRAINER

Quick Tips on How to Teach Others What You Know

C. Leslie Charles
Chris Clarke-Epstein

Dear Jay,

Thank you for your participation.

Congratulations on being a Master Instructor, and on your Mastery of cur/seq & handling problem situations.

Robert Cohen
February 2001

McGraw-Hill

New York   San Francisco   Washington, D.C.   Auckland   Bogotá
Caracas   Lisbon   London   Madrid   Mexico City   Milan
Montreal   New Delhi   San Juan   Singapore
Sydney   Tokyo   Toronto

Library of Congress Cataloging-in-Publication Data

Charles, C. Leslie
    The instant trainer : quick tips on how to teach others what you
know / C Leslie Charles and Chris Clarke-Epstein.
      p. cm.
    Includes index.
    ISBN 0-07-011965-1 (hardcover). — ISBN 0-07-011958-9 (pbk.)
    1. Employee training personnel—Training of.   2. Employees—
Training of.   I. Clarke-Epstein, Chris.   II. Title.
HF5549.5.T7C539   1998
658.3'12404—dc21   97-37422
                                       CIP

McGraw-Hill

A Division of The **McGraw·Hill** *Companies*

ISBN 0-07-011965-1 (h/c) 2 3 4 5 6 7 8 9 0 DOC/DOC 9 0 2 1 0 9
       0-07-011958-9 (s/c)   5 6 7 8 9 0 DOC/DOC   0 2 1 0

*The sponsoring editor for this book was Richard Narramore, the editing supervisor
was Fred Dahl, and the production supervisor was Tina Cameron. This book was set
in Poppl-Laudatio by Inkwell Publishing Services.*

Printed and bound by R.R. Donelley & Sons Company.

For my kindergarten teacher, Mrs. Kiefer, who taught me
that teaching is a glamorous profession,
that learning is fun, and
that I was smart enough to do both.

Chris

To Dave Short who saw my potential,
Tina Kahn who initially trained me,
Cassandra Book who shaped my facilitation skills, and
my trainees who continue to feed my learning curve.

Leslie

CONTENTS

CONTENTS

FOREWORD

Question: What do you get when you take two well-respected trainers, authors, and speakers, and have them create a collection of sage advice especially designed for new or first-time trainers?

Answer: The book you're holding in your hands.

Question: What do you get when these same two trainers and speakers, both members of the American Society for Training and Development, both of whom serve on the National Board of Directors for the National Speakers Association, combine their training expertise, inimitable personalities, professional experience, sense of humor, and practical Midwestern advice?

Answer: The same book you're holding in your hands.

If you're not yet completely intrigued, please read on! Chris Clarke-Epstein and C. Leslie Charles have created a wonderful book for every new or "first-time" trainer or facilitator. In this special "one-stop shopping" resource you will find the equivalent of a seasoned trainer's lifetime of lessons learned. Easy to read and full of personality, the book has the answers to the most often asked questions posed by new trainers and by those who want to maintain their learning curve. And you'll also find some items you haven't even thought to ask.

What will this book do for you? It will help you prevent disasters and apply proven training techniques that will make you look and feel more experienced than you are. Special behind-the-scenes advice will build your confidence and help you avoid the common pitfalls that contribute to poor training. What more could you ask for?

Written with the perfect blend of professionalism and personality by two consummate trainers who earnestly care about your success and that of your learners, *The Instant Trainer* will not only find its place on your trainer's bookshelf, it will find itself in your hands—often! Enjoy.

Edward E. Scannell, CSP
Co-author of *The Games Trainers Play* series
Former President of the American Society for Training and Development,
Meeting Professionals International, and the National Speakers Association

ACKNOWLEDGMENTS

A special thank you to our editor, Richard Narramore, and assistant editor, Mary Loebig-Giles for your wisdom, wit, and endless patience. You answered our naive questions, tolerated our unrestrained enthusiasm, and most of all made us look good with your excellent editing skills. Thank you for everything!

Part I

WHAT EVERY FIRST-TIME TRAINER NEEDS TO KNOW

(Critical Factors That Can Make or Break You!)

INTRODUCTION

***A book, like a training session, needs an opening.
This is ours.***

One day we realized that all the books written to help people deliver good training programs were long and involved. We had a sneaking suspicion that very few people actually read them cover to cover. Sound familiar? You carefully placed those books on your bookshelf to make you look knowledgeable. Maybe you took them home—they ended up on the floor next to your bed and you hoped to get the information by osmosis while you slept. We have tried both of these methods; they don't work.

Becoming a skillful trainer comes from practical experience. That's what this book is all about—sharing the lessons learned during our combined 35 years of training and speaking experiences in a simple, easy-to-read format. You won't find us talking much about the theories our ideas are based on, although in Appendix D we'll give you a list of the books that will. You won't find training ideas that require large budgets or fancy equipment. You won't find complex answers when a simple one will do. You **will** find sensible suggestions that work in the real world. You'll find hints that will make your training sessions more fun for the participants and for you. You'll find insights that might otherwise take years to discover.

We're assuming that you are reading this book because:

- You're a subject matter expert—well versed in your content area but with little or no experience in training others. Many people get thrown into a training position without advance notice and are given a limited amount of time to prepare. Out of nowhere someone says, "Since we've downsized, we need someone who knows a lot about _____ to train the rest of the work team. You fit the bill. I know you can do it."

- You've had a dream of becoming a trainer and you've just made it. Congratulations! You know all the theory and now you get to put it into practice.

- You're an experienced trainer and, like the two of us, can't pass up a new book on training.

- You were inadvertently locked in a training room over a long weekend and you're desperate for something to read.

No matter how you wound up with a training assignment, *The Instant Trainer* will help you plan and prepare better for your training sessions, and keep you from getting too overwhelmed or intimidated by the prospect of teaching others what you know. We'll explain what it takes to create a learning climate and how to identify your participants' wants and needs: who they are, what they already know, what they need to know, and what you can do to gain and hold their attention.

You may have been given the *title* of trainer in an instant, but you can't realistically become an effective trainer in an instant. You will learn, as we have, that successful trainers have made an enormous commitment of time and energy to both their subjects and their deliveries. The lessons we've learned from other exceptional trainers combined with our own lessons (many from the painful process of trial and error) are captured on the pages of this book. Fortunately, you can access them in an instant! While learning from experience is great, you won't always have time for that. Benefiting from other people's experience saves you time and energy, and prevents the anxiety of having to say, "I certainly learned from that!" It's a great way to enhance your knowledge without the pain.

Our job is to help you succeed as a trainer, even on an instant's notice. Just think: Whenever you walk into the classroom you can take *The Instant Trainer* with you. We'll happily share what we know and practice every day. Whatever your topic and wherever you go, you can rest assured that the Instant Trainers will be with you, ready to help. Our intent is to steepen your learning curve—but at a manageable rate so you don't get lost in new information. In our combined 35 years of training, we've discovered a lot about our learners and the art of training. We're happy to pass it on.

HELP! I DON'T KNOW HOW TO TEACH!

Think of all the teachers you've had in your lifetime. Your list will include the ones who bored you to death, who thought yelling would make you learn better, and who never once actually knew your name. You might also remember some teachers who made you think you were a genius, who encouraged your baby steps toward learning something new, and who inspired you to excel. If you were lucky, there were more of the latter than the former. All these teachers shaped how you felt about learning and school—feelings you carry with you today, into each learning situation you encounter.

If memories of your teachers are pleasant, the training assignment that prompted you to pick up this book is probably an exciting one. You'll be able to instruct and inspire the participants in your classes the way your favorite teachers shared new skills and ideas with you. You may be nervous about the responsibility, but you remind yourself, "At least I have good role models to emulate."

On the other hand, you many be worried you'll inflict the same kind of educational pain on others that you had to endure. You wake up in a cold sweat from a nightmare that involves you in the front of a classroom droning on and on and on while students' heads drop to their desks with a series of louder and louder thuds. "Why me," you cry, "why did they ask me to be a teacher?"

No matter which scenario comes closest to your current thoughts and feelings, stop for a minute and consider this. No one asked you to be a **teacher,** nor could you be unless you decided to take time off and head back to school. You've been asked to do something different. You've been asked to share your expertise with people who need to know what you know.

Let's face it. Training an adult, unlike teaching a seven-year-old, could consist of giving a person a book with all the necessary techniques or skills described. You could even make sure there were some pictures in the book for enjoyment. But we doubt much actual learning would take place under those circumstances. That's where you come in. Your role at the front of the room will be to facilitate—to transfer what you know in an orderly, meaningful, and measurable way to the learner. The word *facilitate* comes from the word *facile* which means to make easy, smooth, or simple. That's your job—to make the transfer of learning easier, smoother, and simpler for the learner. You'll accomplish this by sharing all the lessons and shortcuts you've learned over the years. You've already got most of the content you'll ever need.

You've learned that training consists of more than just content. It's not just what you present, it's also **how** you present it. This is the process part. Most people who become trainers in an instant need to spend more than an instant learning how to present what they know. You may have an accounting technique that will simplify a bank teller's closing at the end of the day, but if you can't help the teller understand it, you haven't done your job. You may know how to smooth the ruffled feathers of an upset customer, but if you can't explain your technique, you haven't done your job as a trainer. You may be able to ease the fears of a frightened patient, but if you can't figure out a way for new nurses to practice that skill, you're not doing your job.

So you're not a teacher; you're probably not a full-time trainer, but you are responsible for the learning of others. That's a tall order, but you can fill it if you realize you need to be a student of the training process. Of course, you've already figured that out—that's why you're reading this book!

Before you move on to the next chapter, here are a few things to keep in mind as you start seeing yourself as the facilitator of your participants' learning.

- **Being the expert in the front of the room doesn't mean you know all the answers.** Unlike the grade school teachers we thought knew everything there was to know, those who facilitate adult learners understand they don't need to know all the answers. They do need to find the answers to the questions their participants ask. They also know that for many adult subjects, unlike high school algebra, there is often more than one right answer. Trainers know that adults will often learn better when the process planned by the trainer encourages the learners to find the answers to their own questions.

- **Don't say yes to a training assignment if you're not really comfortable with the content.** Taking on the task of trainer in addition to your regular job responsibilities is a big commitment. If you're being asked to share knowledge and your knowledge level of the subject is minimal at best, you've probably gotten yourself into a tough situation. Even experienced trainers will shy away from an assignment that requires them to learn both brand new content and brand new training skills at once.

- **Approach training as a fun assignment.** No matter what the subject, teachers and trainers who love what they do, do what they do better. Everyone wins when there is an element of enjoyment for both learner and trainer built into a session.

FIVE FACTORS AFFECTING THE SUCCESS OF EVERY TRAINING SESSION

Please Read This Chapter!

If you are tempted to bypass this chapter, please don't! Because training is an awesome responsibility, and because we think you want to do a good job, we recommend you take the time to read all of Part I. Take heart, though; this is the only time we will be so insistent. How you approach the rest of this book is your call (Chapters 11 through 24 are written in a light, question-and-answer format so you can jump around), so please bear with us for now and read on. We will provide you with *instant* information and *brief* bits of practical advice, but first let's get the essentials out of the way before you cruise on.

You've attended training sessions before, right? You can appreciate that adults want the time they spend in a classroom to be worth it, can't you? Take a moment to reflect on some of your most memorable learning experiences as an adult. Were they worthwhile? Enjoyable? Did you receive long-term benefits or did you leave the session resenting the time you wasted? Did you walk away excited because someone ignited a spark within you? You'd like your trainees to feel that way about your sessions, right?

Whether you're brand new to training or bring considerable experience to the training room, it's a demanding job. It helps if you convince yourself that there is some cosmic reason why you've been asked or selected as a trainer, and commit to doing your best.

Your own experiences as a trainee can help you remember the impact you will have on others as the trainer. You know from your own experience that many people have mixed feelings about attending seminars or participating in educational programs. Because people differ in personality, work style, or worldview, some will love the idea of learning or trying something new, and some will hate it. You can probably identify with both. Maybe for you it depends on why you are there, what you are learning, how the material is presented, and what other events are happening in your life. Maybe it depends on who the presenter is.

Today's workforce is filled with active, busy, overcommitted individuals who bring personal issues to the classroom. You will need to command their time and attention, break their preoccupation, and prevent further distractions; never an easy job. But we also know *you* could be experiencing equal pressures, so we will give you as many ideas as we can in the shortest possible amount of time to help make your job easier.

Let's start with the five major factors that can make or break a training session. As you read them, consider which may require your immediate attention.

Beginnings and Endings

Of course, starting out on a positive note makes things easier for you and your learners. This is accomplished when you arrive early, get organized before people arrive, and greet them in a friendly fashion as they enter the room. Later in the book we'll outline simple ways to do just that. Ending with a sense of closure and accomplishment adds a feeling of lasting value for everyone. We'll present you with numerous ways to structure your training sessions and end them in such a way that participants are moved to take action on the information they've learned.

Level of Acquaintance

Training session attendees may or may not know each other. Your hope is that they will get acquainted during the process, but getting classroom participation from your learners is much easier to achieve when they feel comfortable with each other and have a shared experience, even if it's just a simple classroom icebreaker. Occasionally, familiarity can foster competition, resistance, or indifference, but in another section of *The Instant Trainer* we will fill you in on ways to deal with these less than desirable behaviors.

Comfort

People learn best in an environment that is mentally and physically comfortable. We'll outline numerous ways you can create an atmosphere that promotes learning and an open exchange of ideas. Handling these issues, as you can imagine, depends on your attitude and approach. We will encourage you to pay particular attention to room arrangement, temperature, noise control, program structure and format, participation level, and group dynamics.

Educational Level

Unless your workplace is unique, you will have learners with extensive education and some with limited abilities. By varying your presentation methods (rather than relying on just one approach) you'll enhance your capacity for reaching every individual in your audience. We'll offer various methods and approaches to assist learning at all educational and skill levels.

Group Dynamics

People behave differently in groups than they do one-on-one. Now that you're in the front of the room, you'll have the opportunity to learn a lot about human behavior: both your learners' and your own. We'll give you tools for assessing the tone and mood of your group plus strategies for effectively handling some of the more challenging aspects of group dynamics and getting to know yourself better, too.

These five factors affect every audience and every training session. When you attend to these essentials early on, you increase your chances of success. The good news is that you don't have to know (or do) everything at once. You can consult *The Instant Trainer* just-in-time as the need arises!

WHAT'S IN A TRAINING SESSION

Chapter 4

It wasn't just what you said, but how you said it!

All communication operates at two levels: the words we say and how we deliver them. In the training world we use the words *content* (what you say) and *process* (how you say it). In the classroom and outside of it, you've experienced many occasions when people's voice tone or body language said far more than their actual words. Consider your new training role and how your training process might affect the content you are trying to teach.

People will listen to what you say but they'll also take in almost everything you do. Some of your learners will observe your most trivial behavior and attach meaning to it. Their interpretation may be right or wrong. It is important to realize this because they may not say anything to you and you may never realize the significance they attached to your behavior. Here's an example: Leslie once conducted a two-day seminar for a group of social workers in a small town with a largely agricultural population. She had forgotten to bring a second pair of earrings, so she wore the same pair two days in a row. At the end of the session one of the participants asked her if she wore the same earrings two days in a row to test whether anyone would notice! So simply be aware that while people are listening to you, they will be watching you and trying to interpret your actions.

Let's define "content" and "process" in the context of training. *Content* involves the topic you are teaching; the central ideas or skills you're presenting: your agenda, materials, discussion items, problems, ideas, or issues that are raised. Content is the "what" of your session and you'll find yourself spending a lot of time preparing your content.

Process involves not what gets done, but "how" it gets presented, who is involved or left out, the strategies used to get ideas across, and how everyone feels about it. Process involves how you approach your topic, how or when you engage in group discussions or classroom activities, who leads discussions, who contributes (or doesn't), how you stage your breaks, what kind of interplay occurs between you and your participants, how conflict is managed, and generally how your session is structured.

What This Means to You

Most instant trainers spend all their time preparing the content of their training session, and pay little attention to the process parts. As a result, their presentations are often somewhat boring, with little audience interaction. As you present your material, try to lead and encourage discussions, ask and answer questions, and introduce group activities. Here are some considerations about balancing process and content:

1. Prepare your content carefully and blend it with attention to your process. This means you will have a sense of what you want to cover, when you plan to present it, and why. Observe your group at both a content and process level: That is, pay attention not only to what gets said and done, but how it is said and done. This will give you some insights about the dynamics of this particular group.

2. Reflect on your role and style as you begin preparing for your program. Do you tend to be "content" oriented? That is, are you task

focused, time conscious, concerned with results, wanting to stick to the agenda? If so, how can you add process to your structure to give it a needed balance?

3. Or are you more "process" oriented? That is, do you observe the dynamics of how something gets accomplished rather than concerning yourself with getting the job done? Do you pull quiet people into the discussion, observe interchanges, read faces and postures, and note conflicts or personal agendas easily? If so, how can you avoid tangents and ensure that you cover all your material and stick to the time line you've set for yourself?

Good trainers engage their groups in various information gathering, spirited exchanges, and problem-solving activities. Part of your job will be to maintain a balance between the content and process elements of your session, because it takes both to make it all work. Here's a quick review to help you balance content and process:

Content skills involve task-focused activities such as covering a specific topic, completing the agenda, clarifying ideas, keeping discussions on course, honoring time frames, asking and answering questions, offering suggestions, clarifying, summarizing, working toward closure, and taking action after the session.

Process skills include observing people's responses, interpreting remarks, drawing people in on discussions, reading and responding to body language, facial expressions, vocal inflection, and nuances, encouraging participation, defusing or reframing negative remarks, and resolving conflict effectively when it occurs.

Every meeting, briefing, or training session involves both content and process. Each is important, and you want a balance of both. Too much content (task) focus? Group members may walk away frustrated because they feel talked "at" rather than talked "with." They may feel forced or bullied into making a decision they weren't ready for. Too much process? People will feel frustrated with all that discussion and no action! Offer a balance and participants will walk away feeling they got more than they bargained for. And the best part? So will you!

Chapter 5

UNDERSTAND THE PEOPLE YOU'RE TRAINING

Getting to know you, getting to know all about you.

from The King and I

Next time you go to the video store, rent a copy of *The King and I.* In addition to enjoying the story, the dances, and the scenery, listen to the lyrics carefully—especially my favorite song, *Getting to Know You.* Anna, much like you, is nervous about her assignment to teach the children of the King of Siam. She has underestimated the differences between the culture she knows, from her home country of England, and the world she finds herself in, Siam. Everything is strange—the food and the climate, the way people dress and act, what is considered right and wrong. Anna is ready to turn around and go back to the safety of what she knows. Sound familiar? Are you facing your training assignment with the same concerns? Most trainers do at one time or another. They ask themselves, "Who are those people walking into the room and how can I possibly connect with them?" If you face a training session without knowing and verifying some basic facts about your trainees, you're not really prepared.

A side note to those of you who are being asked to train coworkers: Don't fall into the trap of believing that none of this applies to you because you've worked with these people for a long time. That's a dangerous assumption. Even though you work with someone, it does not necessarily follow that you know how they think and feel about learning or about the subject you've been asked to present. Basing your training sessions on things you assume to be true can have surprising ramifications when the training actually begins.

Here are five basic things you must know about your participants before you start to plan your session. The answers to these questions will shape your choices about both what you include in the session (content) and how you present the material you've chosen (process). The time you spend answering these questions will make the rest of your preparation more effective.

- **Who are they?**

  This is a question of demographics. How many men; how many women? What are their average ages? Use a quote from Mary Pickford and watch an under-35-year-old group stare at you with blank expressions. Quote from the rock group U2 and you'll lose the over-55 crowd. What jobs do they do? Will they all know each other or are they strangers? The answers to these and other questions will help you develop a mental picture of the people who will be sitting in your class and determine how you can tailor your presentation to their special needs.

- **Why do they need to learn your subject?**

  Adults learn best when the material they're working on solves a problem they're currently dealing with. If people come to a class without understanding how the new skill or information will help them in their daily lives, the best you can hope for is indifferent learners ("Why bother?"). The worst that can happen will be downright hostile learners ("Why are you taking me away from my real work?"). If the participants don't understand how the material will benefit them, you'll need to establish its relevancy right away.

- **How will they use what they learn about your subject?**

  Right after relevancy comes application. If you don't know how the new skills and information will be used in the participants' workplace, it will be difficult to prepare effective practice sessions for the key points and important techniques. When your examples and exercises ring true in the learners' minds, participants are much more likely to join in and you won't have to spend a lot of time explaining why your material is important.

- **How much do they already know about your subject?**

  Do you have beginners in your class or seasoned veterans? Just before you walk into the training room isn't the time to figure this one out. If you have a combination of both (a common workplace training occurrence) you might need to develop ways to use the more experienced people as coaches while the newer people practice a skill.

- **What do they think of you as their trainer?**

  This may be the toughest question of all. It is often overlooked not only by those who are doing the training, but by those who choose the people to lead the training. Put your ego aside when you go looking for the answer to this question. The answer tells you about the credibility you'll have as you stand in the front of the class. Ironically, this is one place you're apt to score higher than a full-time, professional trainer. If you've built a reputation for doing things well in your organization, people already respect your technical expertise. Sadly, the members of a training department are often perceived as not doing any "real work" (You now know differently, don't you?) and they are not automatically considered experts.

Anna, the teacher in *The King and I,* took the time to learn these and other things about her students. The more she learned about them, the better she was able to reach them, sharing information in ways they could understand. If you take a lesson from Anna, and do your homework—learning about your participants—you and they will have an enjoyable learning experience.

A QUICK LOOK AT ADULT LEARNING THEORY

*Fish **for** me and I eat today. Teach me to fish and I eat forever.*

Chinese proverb

Today's leading-edge organizations are creating environments that support, encourage, and offer ongoing learning in the workplace. In your position as an occasional trainer (or even an experienced one), you are a major player in the learning organization. The better you understand the emotional position of your learners the easier it will be for you to get your message across so that learning occurs. There are special characteristics about adult learners that every trainer needs to consider, especially if you are teaching something your learners may feel resistant about learning.

The hard truth is that no matter how impressive your presentation content or support materials may be, your learners will respond to the intangibles in your presentation such as your attitude, program format, use of time, and overall approach (in other words, *content* is important but *process* often affects how content is perceived and received).

We can explain the principles of adult learning theory briefly and simply, but their skillful application and orchestration can make or break your session. As the trainer, you think your program is important and that everyone should listen up, but today's learners are busy. Their personal and work time is fragmented and some people resent spending time in training sessions; they think it keeps them from doing their jobs. We need to change people's perceptions and help them understand that learning is as much a legitimate part of their work as is classroom time.

Let's take a quick look at adult learning theory as originally conceived by Malcolm and Hulda Knowles. Their theory is as applicable today as it was when introduced many years ago. We've recapped their major points and added our own comments in italics:

- Adult learners come to a presentation with some set notions and expectations. Some had bad experiences in school and if they rarely attend training sessions, they may be apprehensive and uncomfortable. *Do what you can to set positive expectations so people can relax and settle in early on. Your efforts to establish a comfortable climate, clarify expectations, explain your agenda, and outline events will help your learners prepare themselves for learning.*

- Adult learners have other important things they could be doing and you are competing with many real-life concerns. Today's workers balance multiple professional roles and personal concerns such as health, child care, parent care, debt, and conflicting relationships. *You need to break through their preoccupation and help them understand that what you are teaching will directly benefit them. Between complicated work and personal demands, people have short attention spans. You need to get their attention and make it all worthwhile.*

- Adult learners are interested in practicality and benefits. People are too busy to care about theory and conjecture. They want concrete, realistic, do-able practices. *Offer practical options and workable approaches to common problems and you'll keep people's attention. Every now and then, let people know how they will benefit from what you're teaching them. Answer the question, "What's in it for me?"*

- Adult learners bring a variety of experiences to the classroom. People will be more interested in what you have to offer them if you can make it relevant to their experience and orientation. *People will be more inclined to listen and learn if you make it a point to speak their language and align your material with their experience. Your responsibilities include developing ways for your learners to use their own personal experiences as a learning resource.*

- Adult learners bring a variety of attitudes to the classroom. Generally speaking, the people who least need the training will be the most receptive toward it and those who most need your message will resist it. *You will maintain more credibility and influence if you are able to operate independently of people's negative attitudes. Your neutrality and acceptance of their situation often has more of a positive influence than all the persuasion you could muster.*

- Adult learners want and expect to be treated with respect and they respond to an environment that encourages learning. People need to feel emotionally comfortable in your session, secure in knowing they will not be singled out, belittled, or intimidated in any way. *You want to enjoy your training sessions and you want your learners to enjoy the process, too. Common courtesy sets the stage for a productive learning environment that offers comfort, variety, and positive reinforcement.*

Just for fun, here's a poem on Adult Learning Theory:

Learners need a comfortable environment:
Challenge their minds, not their behinds.

Learners want practical information they can apply immediately:
If you offer an early solution, they'll stay with you till the conclusion.

Learners want to use their past experiences as a resource:
If you build on what they know, your credibility will grow.

Learners want information specifically related to them:
Relevant is the magic word that helps ensure that you'll be heard.

Learners want variety and active involvement when learning:
A little bit of lecture is nice but activities give your training spice.

Learners want and need to be respected:
Yes, your learners learn from you; but you learn from your learners, too.

Learner motivation is affected by outside concerns:
Adult learners have other things on their minds, but if you keep it fun they'll leave their cares behind!

GROUP DYNAMICS

"The whole is greater than the sum of the parts."

How people learn in a group is a complex topic and many books have been written on the subject. But because we are Instant Trainers, here is the condensed version of what happens when people form into groups. You've probably noticed that each group tends to take on its own personality. How a group of employees from the same organization behaves usually reflects the organizational culture, whatever that may be. A group of strangers tends to develop its own style as people get acquainted.

Some groups are fun-loving and expressive, some are quiet and reflective. The people in some groups laugh easily and are extremely playful or responsive, while other groups have members who simply smile and nod. And some groups are downright resistant. It's fascinating how a collection of individuals takes on a collective personality.

One excellent model of group dynamics is entitled "Tuckman's Development Sequence," which describes four stages of group development. As you read the stages, consider what is happening at both an interpersonal realm (process) and task level (content). Here is the model:

Stage One: Forming

People begin learning how the group will operate, noting what behaviors are acceptable or unacceptable, who the emerging leaders are, and how the trainer relates to the group (and vice versa). Behavioral guidelines establish the groundwork for how information will be presented, sought after, and handled.

Stage Two: Storming

In this stage, there is little unity. Status levels begin forming and power struggles may emerge between the trainer and group members, or among group members themselves. People try to express their individuality and establish themselves within the group. There may be some resistance to task demands if people are unclear about what is expected of them.

State Three: Norming

This is the stage in which group members become more accepting of each other. Group norms solidify and people become more accepting of their differences. With effective leadership, harmony replaces hostility. The energy initially expended through tension and self-expression now converts into open discussion, exchange of ideas, and expression of opinions within the group.

Stage Four: Performing

In this stage group members are ready to roll up their sleeves and work. They've gotten past most of the relationship issues, established a semblance of interdependence, and can now focus on their tasks. Problem solving and group projects can be completed with little disagreement or dissension.

Tuckman's model eloquently describes the process of group formation and you'll observe some or all of these dynamics in almost any interactive training session that lasts one day or longer. Keep in mind that in real life, progression through these stages is not linear. Groups will move from one stage to another and back again, depending on the circumstances. For example, Stages Two and Three are interchangeable, depending on the personalities in the group, the nature of the task, and the style of the trainer.

Understanding these stages of group development can be helpful, particularly if someone turns on you during the Storming stage. This way, you don't have to take it personally and wonder if there were something you could have done or said to avoid it.

As you can imagine, it's the Storming stage that can solidify a group. Think of a time when you were in a group and substantive issues got laid on the table, discussed in depth, and resolved. Open exchange such as this helps a group congeal.

Not every group goes through these four stages. You may zip through a short meeting and witness little or no dynamics. How long the group will exist and why they are together are factors that influence group dynamics, though certainly individual personalities are another factor.

If your session involves problem solving or creating a group outcome, here are four strategies you can employ to ease group members through the development stages and help them transform into positive, productive learners:

1. *Set the stage*—Establish the environment, outline the agenda, establish guidelines, explain the task at hand, observe group norms that emerge, and explain the process. Help people get acquainted, break the ice, note individual differences, allow differences to surface, and establish an atmosphere of openness and acceptance.

2. *Minimize conflict*—Let group members know that while differing opinions and divergent styles are welcome, open competition is undesirable because it interferes with creative problem solving.

3. *Elicit group input*—Pose questions, ask for feedback, encourage participation, solicit ideas, and prepare the group for problem solving. Encourage people to take turns talking and openly listen to the ideas of others.

4. *Address the task*—State problems, redefine issues, establish priorities, identify options, summarize suggestions, and submit potential solutions. Observe and evaluate the outcome, let group members know how their input is being used, celebrate the end result, evaluate the process, and make course corrections when necessary.

Odd things can happen when people get into groups, but you can prevent some harmful incidents from occurring. If you ever anticipate conflict or power struggles with a particular group, ask them to establish behavioral guidelines before they begin. They're far more likely to honor their own guidelines than yours. This is one way of lessening the intensity of the Storming stage so you can move on to the stage where things get done: Performing.

Chapter 8

TRAINERS WHO PAY ATTENTION

*See with your heart, listen with your eyes,
and feel with your sense of humor.*

If you've ever wondered what a trainer needs to monitor the most, you could summarize it in one word: everything. Indeed, there are a myriad of details you'll need to oversee, but managing them is easier than you think. With experience, most trainers develop a sixth sense for what needs to be done. They use all of their faculties to observe, interpret, and respond to whatever the group needs at a given time. Here are the factors that experienced, effective trainers pay attention to. With a little bit of practice you, too, can cultivate these capabilities.

Good trainers keep track of time. If you don't work in a room with a clock, you'll want to have your own. If you do work in a room with a clock, it's best if you can see it but your participants can't. By the way, having a clock is different from having a watch if you didn't catch the distinction. If you check your watch, your participants will check theirs, too. A clock well-positioned on the wall or your table helps you keep track of time without having to distract your learners. Your ability to manage classroom time enhances your credibility: Start on time and end on time and you will look like a pro.

Effective trainers monitor the room temperature. Hot or cold, the show must go on, but it's nice if the room temperature is as close to ideal as possible. That's one of the advantages of arriving early; you can adjust the temperature before people arrive. A collection of adults in a small room can warm it up, so keep that in mind as you adjust the thermometer. Once you get rolling, if the air becomes too warm or too cool, do something about it. Even if you can't change the temperature in the room, if your learners witness you trying to, they will be impressed with your efforts.

Seasoned trainers closely watch people's facial expressions and body language. You can probably trust your instincts as to what people are thinking or feeling by the looks on their faces. If you see a few people wearing the same expression, stop and check it out. In particular, look for frowns, questioning looks, nods of affirmation, or shakes of disagreement. On the other hand, seeing absolutely no expression can mean that people either don't understand what you've said or their collective energy level has hit the wall and you need to wake them up.

Teach yourself to watch what people do with their bodies. Slumping, slouching, and fidgeting can be indicators of fatigue or boredom and a sign to switch gears. Excessive side discussions may signal the need to get people into groups for a few moments, or initiate a discussion. It could also mean you've stepped onto sensitive ground. Usually there is more than one indicator to help you figure out what's going on with your group. Watch faces and postures, and how people treat each other. Listen for sighs or other sounds that may mean fatigue, frustration, or disagreement. Respond to these behaviors positively and appropriately; then even if you need to confront someone, you can do so tactfully.

Experienced trainers pay attention to group interaction and know how to read the cues. Determine how comfortable people are when interacting with each other or when communicating with you. Note how group members respond when certain individuals speak or ask a question. Pay attention to how many people in your group are actively involved and how many choose not to participate. Consider what kinds of questions get asked or the nature of comments people make during discussions. You can learn a lot about a group's personality by paying attention to how people interrelate with each other and you.

Good trainers monitor participation levels and do their best to achieve a high level of participation. When you ask a question, note how long it takes for someone to respond, and if it's the same person all the time. When you ask learners to discuss an issue, note whether they actually follow your directions. By encouraging everyone to get actively involved in the learning process, you can create a highly participative, productive environment.

Excellent trainers develop a "feel" for when it's time to switch gears, move on, go more in-depth, or add a splash of humor. Call them intuitive, experienced, observant, omniscient, or whatever, they just *know.* You can do that too, by using your observation skills and responding to your group in an appropriate fashion. No, this special skill doesn't develop overnight, and some of us are naturally better at it than others, but you'll be surprised at what a quick study you are. We know that even new trainers can observe a particular behavior and respond to it instantly and appropriately!

Chapter 9

RED LIGHTS, GREEN LIGHTS: EARLY WARNING SIGNS OF DISASTER OR SUCCESS

Danger, danger, Will Robinson!

said by the Robot in every episode of Lost in Space

As experienced drivers, we all know to ease off the gas when we see a squad car in the rearview mirror, whether we're speeding or not. It's a built-in reflex from years of seeing lights flashing in the distance, passing cars pulled over on the side of the road, and catching quick glimpses of drivers meekly accepting a ticket. We drive on, grateful that we saw the squad car, otherwise occupied, before it saw us!

It would be great if there were the equivalent of flashing lights for trainers to alert us when things aren't working out. Just as helpful would be some signals to encourage us when our programs are right on track. Here is the Instant Trainers' list of early warning—disaster and success—

signs. When you encounter one, follow the advice you got from your Mom, your teachers, and Officer Friendly—stop, look, and listen. You'll be glad you did!

You're facing trouble if ...

- **You're not engaged**

  If you find yourself without any butterflies before a session, watch out. A little bit of nervousness signals you that you're engaged and ready to do a great job. The absence of a small nervous reaction may mean that you're not fully committed to your training assignment. If you're not deeply involved in what you are about to do, don't expect your participants to be.

- **Your credibility is in question**

  If you approach a training assignment and you have the feeling that the participants have doubts about your ability to draw on personal experience as you discuss your topic, beware. Think about it. You wouldn't want to learn golf from someone who never held a golf club, or learn customer service from someone who has never had to deal with a cranky customer. If you have expertise in your subject but the trainees are unaware of it, you need to establish your credentials early on.

  If you've been asked to lead a session and your content knowledge comes from books rather than experience, you've got a bigger problem. The truth is, you may not be the right person to do the job. If you can't appropriately back out of the assignment, maybe you can find a partner with the practical experience to balance your theory and do a team presentation.

- **You've lost control of the group, the environment, or the material**

  If you realize one of the participants is monopolizing the class conversations, if the room is too hot or too cold, or if an activity you planned just isn't working, find an appropriate place to call a short break. Head to the bathroom and lock yourself in a stall (yes, you will have to come back out!) and mentally take back control of your session. Decide what you're going to do differently and do it. In *The Instant Trainer* you'll find great solutions to these and other common training situations. You need to realize it is your responsibility to do something and do it **now**! Participants have the right to expect that you'll control the flow of the session, the environmental factors that influence their ability to learn, and the appropriateness of the material.

Your training is working when ...

- **People laugh easily**

  Watch people's actions, expressions, and energy level as they enter the classroom. If, during the first ten minutes of your session, they become animated, smile or chuckle a bit, and perk up, you can be sure you're off to a good start. Learning is a very satisfying activity and, as with all pleasing endeavors, people's attitudes improve as they do them.

- **Everyone participates with enthusiasm**

  Watch how people participate in the activities you've planned. Participation, in and of itself, isn't an accurate measure of success. You may be higher on the organizational totem pole and participation may be motivated by fear of reprisal. Your corporate culture may dictate activity. However, **eager** participation indicates a self-motivated learner. When you're in a classroom of self-motivated learners, you're in trainer's heaven!

- **People complete evaluation forms with comments**

  There is a book called *The Gift of Feedback: Dealing with Customer Complaints.* Sometimes when you start reading a stack of evaluation forms, the feedback won't feel like much of a gift. But think about it. You've been given a gift when participants are willing to take one of their most precious possessions, their time, and spend it giving you the supportive and sometimes critical information you need to improve your presentation. They have told you that they cared enough about your session (and you) to give you information you can work with rather than a few meaning-less check marks on a scale of 1 to 10. We'd rather have an evaluation form that rates our program a 7 with written explanations of what we did right and what needs some work, than a 9 with no comments.

Chapter 10

HOW TO READ THE REST OF THIS BOOK

Since you've read this far, raise your right hand, drop it over your left shoulder, and give yourself a pat on the back! The rest of the book is designed to provide information on demand. You can, of course, read it page by page, but we thought you'd be more likely to use it as an instant advisor, providing just-in-time assistance.

Part II of *The Instant Trainer* contains 14 mini-chapters, each dealing with a critical aspect of training, written in an easy-to-read question and answer format. At the beginning of each chapter there's a short essay that will tell you why we've chosen to cover that subject. Then you'll find a series of questions and answers about issues relating to that subject. By reading the questions, you'll be able to decide whether or not you need the information in the answer.

Skip around. Read the parts that are important to you now. Peruse the sections that pique your interest. Ignore the ones that cover experiences you've had or skills you've learned.

Keep this book handy. Use it to gain new perspectives on old problems. Write in the margins. Dog-ear the pages that feature points you want to remember.

If your question isn't answered in the first 90 percent of this book, turn to the end of Chapter 24 to discover how you can have your question answered personally by the authors. Our commitment as the Instant Trainers is to answer your question in as close to an instant as we can!

Part II

QUESTIONS AND ANSWERS ON TRAINING BASICS

PREPARING YOURSELF

You're experienced in this stuff. You can run the class next week.

*overheard, with increasing frequency,
in workplaces around the globe.*

So, somebody decided you should be the trainer. Whether you're excited about the opportunity or dreading the task, you've got to start somewhere. We know you want to do a good job when you're the one standing in the front of the room. But wanting and doing aren't necessarily the same thing. Training is no different from any other profession; there are tricks to the trade. That's what *The Instant Trainer* is all about—tips that will help you be a better trainer in an instant.

The tips start with preparing yourself. Good trainers know they need to tend to themselves so they can tend to their learners. It's usually the star athletes that show up early for training camp. The best musicians practice the most. Or, as Jack Nicklaus put it, "The harder I prepare, the luckier I get." Good trainers aren't good by luck or accident. They work at being ready, paying attention to the little details that can make or break a training session.

If you're faced with the need to become a trainer in an instant, this section will help you think about some of the details before **not** thinking about them becomes a problem. From being honest about the butterflies that seem to take up residence in your stomach before any presentation, to deciding what supplies you'll need for the activities you've planned, you'll find the answers here. In fact, we'll give you answers to questions you haven't even thought to ask yet.

Remember, when you invest some of your time in organizing yourself, your equipment, and your materials, you can turn your attention to the really important part of a training session—the learners.

Dear Instant Trainers:

My boss has asked me to demonstrate our new software to my work team. If this goes well, I may be asked to repeat the presentation for everyone in our manufacturing company (we have nearly 1800 employees). As a brand new trainer, I want to start out right and not have to make a fool of myself the first time I get up in front of the group, especially because many of these people know me. I realize you can't produce instant miracles, but are there two or three things I can do my first time out that might give my trainees the feeling that I know what I'm doing?

Rookie in Rochester

Dear Rookie:

Well, we all have to start somewhere. There's an old saying attributed to Dorothy Sarnoff: Preparation compensates for a lack of talent. The first way to protect your credibility is through careful preparation. Know your software in and out. Read up on it. Work with the package so you know the positives and negatives. Talk with the software company's technical support crew and request any additional support literature they may have. Develop a special Q & A series and include it as part of your training session. If no short-cuts or tip sheets accompany the software package, create one. This way you become an instant expert on your topic.

The other aspect of preparation involves how you organize your material. Create a logical flow or sequence for teaching the entire package, from why the software exists to what it will do for the user and how. Make notes so you'll remember to include those incidental "by the way" tips, and don't be afraid to use them. Practice, practice, practice. Do a few dry runs. When the day comes for your first presentation, get there early so everything is set up and organized before anyone else arrives. This gives you the opportunity to welcome and chat with people as they come in. Relax and remind yourself that many of your participants will be more nervous than you! If you have the time or inclination, read what the Instant Trainers have to say about delivery skills or posture and gestures in Chapter 17. Other than that, relax, have fun, and make the process enjoyable for yourself and your learners. It might help to remind yourself that every pro, in every worthwhile endeavor, was once a rookie, too.

Leslie

Dear Rookie:

Leslie's right. The difference between simply doing something and doing it well is preparation! Here's what I'd focus on first: What do your learners want and need to know the most about this software program? If you find out the answers to this question and focus on sharing this information early in your program, you'll have motivated learners! To find out what's important to your learners, ask them. You can do this informally, with a brief questionnaire, or convene a small focus group and lead a discussion. By adding this step to your preparation, you'll know your material will be targeted correctly (and so will your learners).

Chris

 Dear Instant Trainers:

I have been recruited to present a product demo to one of our major clients. As a technician (as opposed to a sales representative) this is not usually my job. Demonstrations are usually the realm of salespeople, but because this client's concern is equipment reliability, my manager thought it would be good if someone with technical expertise went along. Well, I do have the expertise, but the last time I was asked to speak in front of people was in high school speech class and I blew it. Our group will be small, maybe five people, but so far that doesn't give me much comfort. Can you give me a crash course on how to get through the demo without passing out?

Choked in Charleston

Dear Choked:

First of all, take a nice, deep breath. Breathe in through your nose, fill your diaphragm with nice clean, energizing air, and then breathe out through your mouth and let your tension leave your body along with that old, used air. It's a small group and remember, you can only speak to one person at a time. You know your products. You know your reliability statistics. You know what your clients need to hear. Focus on the importance of your information and concentrate on giving your clients what they need to make a buying decision. Focus is the operative word, okay?

Prepare. Know what you are going to say and when. Coordinate your words with your demo techniques and strategies. If you and your sales rep will be working together, organize yourselves and do a dry run ahead of time. If you need notes, use them. A handout of reliability statistics could be a nice souvenir for your small audience and you could highlight the critical information for them.

Even in a small group you can speak to only one person at a time. Just have a conversation. Look each person in the eye, especially when making an important point. Give the group directions from time to time. Examples: "Let me demonstrate for you ..." or, "If I can walk you through this particular function for a moment...." This will keep people focused on what you want them to hear, see, and learn. Smile when you make a point that directly benefits the client. Pause between sentences and avoid speaking too rapidly.

The information on posture and gestures in Chapter 17 will give you some good tips. Keep your hands relaxed, or at least make them look relaxed. Wear something that both looks good on you and feels good to you. If you feel comfortable, you'll look comfortable to your clients. These few hints will keep you from choking, and instead you can charm your audience with all of the capabilities of your products (and yourself)!

Leslie

Dear Choked:

Does it help to know that you're not alone? You'd be amazed how many people share your fear of speaking in front of groups. Here's another idea you can try. First, meet with the salesperson and ask her or him for a description of the people who will attend the meeting. By visualizing them as individuals rather than as a group, you'll be able to think, "I'm talking to a him or a her, rather than a unknown them." Make certain you get to the meeting early, introduce yourself to each participant, shake hands, and make eye contact. When you stand up to speak, you'll be amazed how different you'll feel as you look into the faces of people you know, rather than looking out on an unknown audience.

Chris

Dear Instant Trainers:

Our training coordinator is off on maternity leave and I've been asked to fill in while she is gone. Next week we have a management class scheduled and I've been asked to lead it. This is a licensed program with video tapes, workbooks, and a leader's guide, so I'm not completely on my own, but I have never done anything like this before, and there's no one to train me. Should I be up front and let people know I'm not the person who usually does this or should I try to fake it? Will I totally lose credibility if I explain I'm just a replacement or am I worse off if I don't tell them? I hope it's evident that I am more than willing to step in; I just don't know for sure the best way to handle my temporary training role.

Game in Galveston

Dear Game:

As you can imagine, there are many schools of thought regarding how one handles being the temporary in-house trainer. I subscribe to the open and honest approach. (I think it was Mark Twain who said if you tell the truth you don't have to remember as much.) If you explain that you volunteered or were invited to operate as the temporary trainer, I think you will actually gain credibility. Considering how most people feel about public speaking, who in your audience would want to be in your shoes? People want to feel they are receiving a quality learning experience, even with a temporary trainer, so it would be good for you to let everyone know you plan to do your absolute best. Your positive attitude will convince them you mean every word.

Preparation will be critical. Review your leader's guide. Review participant materials. And preview each video segment before your program so you're not taken off guard by any of the content. Many fledgling professors and trainers use the approach of staying one lesson ahead of their students, and you can do the same.

Make notes in your leader's guide or your own copy of the materials so you can add personal comments and instructions. Practice operating the VCR and any other equipment you'll be using. Make sure the room setup is conducive to your purpose. Determine if everyone will be able to see the monitor and whether the room is set up for discussion if that's an important part of the process. Write down a series of questions in your notes that will keep things moving in case you have a quiet group. Then just sit back (or stand) and let each meeting unfold like a good card hand, one session at a time. If you're game to try all of these strategies, we think your group will be willing to follow suit.

Leslie

Dear Game:

Our parents were right—honesty is the best policy. As you briefly explain the circumstances that have brought you to the front of the room, include a few words to let your learners know you've done all the things Leslie suggested. You want to be certain that participants understand that while you may be a temporary trainer, your commitment to their learning experience is permanent!

Chris

 Dear Instant Trainers:

In three days I will give my first presentation, and as you can imagine I'm pretty nervous about it. I've done my homework, read a few books, prepared my materials, and feel as if I've learned as much as I can without actually getting my feet wet. I would like to know if there is anything else I can do to help myself appear more experienced than I am, so people will have confidence in me. What are some of the things experienced pros do (or don't do) to give them that air of confidence?

Winging it in Wahpeton

Dear Winging it:

Well, you can feel better already, because you're not really winging it. You've done a lot of homework and gone beyond the realm of the usual neophyte. As you asked, here are a few "secrets of the pros" that will give your confidence a boost.

If you have any handouts or prepared information to distribute, make sure you have enough for everyone. Always carry a few extras. Know how to operate whatever equipment you plan to use. Work with it ahead of time.

Open your program with something more stimulating than the standard welcome and administrivia (break times, logistics, and other details can be covered a few minutes later). Get there early enough so you can be all set up and organized before the first person comes in. Personally welcome people as they arrive.

Here's one that only seasoned trainers know: Avoid using collective nouns ("Now, group …"). Keep in mind you are working with a group of **individuals,** not just a group. Set your room up in other than classroom style and right away you will look like a pro (and maybe feel more like it, too). Sprinkle in a bit of humor (cartoons are great), let people know that fun is a part of learning, practice the confident body language mentioned in Chapter 17, and just be yourself.

Put a small clock on your head table so you can keep track of time without having to look at your watch. Start on time, end on time, and take your breaks on time. If time runs short, rather than trying to cover ten pages in ten minutes, pick out the most important element (this is part of your preparation) and explain to your trainees that the rest of the material can be covered after the program. Pros (experienced trainers) always identify their Key Points ahead of time so they will know when to hold 'em and when to fold 'em if time runs short. Even if you're rushed, don't give that appearance. Speak in your same cadence and rhythm, and breathe! These tips will make you look like a pro and help your training skills soar in a short amount of time.

Leslie

Dear Winging it:

Congratulations! You've really done your homework. All of the prep work you've done has, by necessity, emphasized you—what you are going to say, what order you are going to do it in, what you are going to wear—you get the idea. Now that you've done all that preparation, there's another step I'd like to suggest: Forget about yourself and think about the participants.

If you bring an attitude of caring about your students to the front of the room, your focus will be in the right place. Your participants will feel it and will respond in kind. Remember, training isn't about how good the trainer is, it's about how much the learner learns. In my experience, the trainers who understand this simple fact are always great!

Chris

Dear Instant Trainers:

I think I could be a good trainer. The branch manager at our bank has asked me to train some of the new tellers. I was amazed to discover I really enjoyed the experience. And don't tell anyone, but I really liked school. My problem is that when I even think about getting up in front of a group of people, I break out in a cold sweat! I'd really like to do the training without all the anxiety. Can you help me?

Nervous in Nantucket

Dear Nervous:

There are stories of very famous actors, musicians, and speakers who, after years of performing, still experience major attacks of nerves. Sweaty palms, a dry mouth, or a stomach full of butterflies are all signals of your body going into overdrive as your concern about doing a good job heightens.

Much of the nervousness you're experiencing comes from putting your focus in the wrong place—on yourself. As long as the voice in your head is saying things like, "I hope I don't say anything dumb!" or "What if I forget a main point?" or "Why did I ever say I'd do this?" you're bound to be nervous. If you put the focus in the right place—on the learners—your anxiety level is bound to go down. When the refrain changes to something like "I wonder how the trainees are feeling about this class?" and "The information I have to share will really help people," you'll be amazed how the nervousness settles down.

In addition to checking your focus, there are several things you can do to help yourself lessen the butterflies.

- Cut down on your caffeine. Coffee, sodas, and tea will add to your jitters. Lowering your intake before the session will moderate the effect of the caffeine.

- Get to your room with plenty of time to spare. Rushing to get your materials set up before the participants arrive does nothing to settle your nerves. Having enough time to deal with any unforeseen issues keeps your anxiety to a minimum.

- Figure out a way to have a few minutes to yourself shortly before the session starts. The easiest way is to make a quick trip to the rest room, lock the door, and take a few deep breaths.

- Know what you're going to say first. I never advise people to memorize their material—with the exception of the first sentence. I find comfort from knowing the exact words that will come out of my mouth when it's lights, camera, action!

Ironically, it has been my experience that once you get nervousness before a session under control, there's another, potentially bigger problem— if you're not a little nervous you're not engaged enough! But then you didn't ask that question!

Chris

Dear Nervous:

It might help to think of your nervousness as extra energy that will help sustain you during your session. One of the biggest mistakes people make is fighting this energy surge instead of accepting it. So rather than beating yourself up for feeling some level of anxiety, accept it as an indicator that you're about to venture into new territory. You're about to do something new, something you're not accustomed to doing. Accepting this reality can make a big difference in how you feel. In time, conducting a training session will begin to feel more comfortable and so will that feeling of nervousness that comes over you before you begin. Yes; you'll adjust. In fact, you may never get over that feeling of anxiety before you begin, but you can get used to it! If you stay focused on your purpose and on how your program will benefit your participants, you'll find you feel less stressed. Just as world-class athletes prepare for their events, you can approach your training sessions with the same attitude. It's called letting your stress work for you, not against you. You'll be amazed at all of the other areas of your life to which this principle will apply!

Leslie

 ### Dear Instant Trainers:

I work at our local United Way agency.

I just finished my first all-day training session for our volunteers. I was the trainer and I'm exhausted! I can't believe some people do this day after day. How can you take care of yourself, keep your attention focused, and conserve your energy during a long training program?

Tired in Tucson

Dear Tired:

Welcome to the hardest part of training! I've come to believe that getting ready for a long training session is like preparing to run a marathon. In addition to getting your content and materials ready, you need to prepare yourself physically.

Nothing will help your stamina and energy level better than a daily dose of physical activity. I know this and sometimes practice it; Leslie knows it and practices it! So, I'm going to let Leslie give you some pointers that you can use to get and keep yourself in top physical shape because she's my hero and my coach when it comes to daily exercise.

What I can share are a few tips I've gathered over the years that tend to **your** creature comforts during a long training session:

- Eat a good breakfast. Not exactly new advice, but it does apply.

- Eat a light lunch. Nothing's worse than the trainer yawning an hour after a heavy meal!

- Drink water. After the coffee you need to get going (if you do need your A.M. shot of java), switch to water. Skip the ice—it does bad things to your vocal cords. In addition to all the good things the water will do for your system, it will remind you to call regular breaks!

- Spend a few minutes outside during the day. Often it's hard to sneak outside (not to mention get to the bathroom) during a break. You'll be busy getting materials ready and talking to participants, so make sure you take the time to get out into the fresh air during your lunch break. You can recharge your energy, attitude, and focus with a few deep breaths of fresh air.

- Wear well-fitted shoes. When you're standing, especially on carpet over concrete floors, the first thing that will go is your feet. A quality pair of real leather shoes is a good investment. Some of my trainer friends swear by the gel-filled inserts you can find at Sharper Image, some use good old Dr. Scholl's—experiment to find the ones that work for you. Try changing your shoes midway through the session. When I do a day's worth of training I always tuck a second pair of shoes in my bag. You'll be amazed how much comfortable feet can improve your attitude.

As you prepare yourself for a training session, don't forget to spend some time thinking about what you need to do for you. A tired, cranky, or listless trainer isn't likely to deliver a first-rate training session.

Chris

Dear Tired:

Indeed, a full day of training can be a real challenge to your energy level, but there are some measures you can take to pace yourself. Chris is right about exercise being important; if you're in good shape you'll feel less fatigued at the end of the day. Even if you're not a major athlete, you can benefit from a regular exercise program. The ideal exercise mix consists of three factors: strength, endurance, and flexibility. These translate into a regimen of muscle toning, aerobics, and stretching. Toned muscles help your posture; you can stand on your feet longer without feeling as if you need a hot tub. A strong heart helps your respiration and ability to stand, move, and speak with less fatigue. And flexibility means you have increased mobility and range of motion.

If you are unable to run, walk, or engage in heart-pumping exercises on the days you find yourself in front of a group, at least work the other two exercise elements into your routine. Yoga is a wonderful option for combining stretching and strengthening at the same time.

Another great option for energy management is to create a "time out" for yourself so you can spend ten to twenty minutes of relaxation (or meditation) before your session. It will help you get centered and recharged. For me, the idea of getting outside is nice, but if I go out I'll want to walk and expend more energy. I'm more likely to find a quiet spot in which I can take a meditation break during my lunch hour when working a full day.

The best of all worlds is that you begin taking such good care of yourself during a training day that you begin to practice the same habits on the days you're not training.

Leslie

 Dear Instant Trainers:

I'm really new at this training stuff and the room that we use for training at our food processing plant is often used for other things. I have to bring equipment and materials for each session. It occurred to me that there are probably some supplies I should always have with me, no matter what the subject of the session is. What tools of the training trade do you think I should have?

Tool-less in Toledo

Dear Tool-less:

I'm so glad you asked! For years I spent time searching for, begging the loan of, and bemoaning the absence of things I needed in the training room. I must be a slow learner, because it seemed forever before it occurred to me that I could come up with a list of necessities, put them in a kit and bring them to every training session I did. It worked—no more last-minute, frantic searching for me! Here's what my kit contains:

> A roll of masking tape
>
> A pair of scissors
>
> A small Swiss Army knife
>
> Two sets of overhead markers—one permanent, one washable
>
> Assorted flip chart markers (none of which are the stinky kind)
>
> Several small noisemakers
>
> Several sharpened pencils
>
> Several pens
>
> Assorted color Post-it note pads
>
> A stapler with extra staples
>
> A few rubber bands
>
> A few paper clips
>
> Some thumbtacks or push pins
>
> Some aspirin and Imodium AD (Can you guess why these are included?)

I keep my kit in an inexpensive cloth cassette carrying case that I found at a discount store. I just removed the plastic form that holds the cassettes and it became a perfect soft-sided, easily packed, handle provided carrying bag. If you go looking for one you might want to choose the larger size; your list of necessities may be longer than mine.

One final hint. Discipline yourself to replenish your kit after every session. As trainers, we tend to have exceptional memories; they are, however, often short! Just yesterday I opened my kit to grab the masking tape so I could hang some flip charts … I bet I don't have to tell the rest of the story!

Chris

Dear Tool-less:

Here are a few additional items for your trainer's necessity kit. The items marked with a box (■) are only for the occasions when I will be using an overhead projector.

A three-prong adapter

A rubber door stop (I'm amazed at how often I use this!)

A fingernail file

Butterscotch hard candies or cough drops

Facial tissues

Transparent tape

An 8 1/2 × 11 note pad

A small digital clock that lies flat

■ *Blank overhead transparencies*

■ *A heavy-duty extension cord*

■ *My Instaframe*

It's a good feeling when you have a need for an item, you open up your trainer's kit, and there it is! It is a bad feeling when you kick yourself for forgetting an obvious necessity. Keeping your kit packed up and ready to go takes you one step closer to being an effective trainer. If you want to go from effective to excellent trainer, browse through Chapter 12, on room setup and logistics. You might find some other tips there.

Leslie

 Dear Instant Trainers:

When my sergeant asked me to put together a program on personal safety for some local civic groups, I didn't think it was a big deal. Getting the material together wasn't hard. I've talked about these issues since my first day as a cop. What I never expected was how much time it takes to get ready for a program. It seems as though I'm always adding, subtracting, or forgetting something. Can you help?

Unorganized in Urbana

Dear Unorganized:

Since I'm writing this on a plane, I have to give the pilots the credit for my answer. If you peek into the cockpit as you board a flight, you'll notice the flight crew busily working through their preflight checklists. Years of doing a job can lull you into a false sense of security. An "oh, I'll never forget to put the flaps in the takeoff position" attitude can be very dangerous. So they leave nothing to chance and follow their checklists.

Here are some ideas for checklists you may want to develop for yourself. Once you do put one together, use it a few times and see if it works the way you want it to. If it does, print up a bunch and discipline yourself to use them. If it doesn't, revise it and try again until it meets your needs. (Look at the sample checklists in Appendix A. You can use them to get started.)

A People Checklist

There are some basic things you need to know about the people in your session, from their ages to their attitudes. Knowing your audience is one of the most important elements in making certain your material is suitable.

A Place Checklist

Getting your room set up right is often a critical factor in the success of your training session. If your session is being held in a hotel or community facility, a place checklist will remind you to ask the right questions when you talk to your facilities contact. If you are using a room in your own facility, it will remind you of what you'll need to do to before the session. For further information on setting up your room, you might want to read the questions and answers in Chapter 12, Dealing with the Logistics.

A Materials Checklist

If you distribute materials, handouts, or job aids or need markers, Post-it notes, or scissors for each participant, a materials checklist will help you avoid having more people than paper. This list is especially helpful if you are fortunate enough to have someone who will help you get ready for your session. Using a materials checklist will help you communicate clearly.

A Content Checklist

This checklist will help you save preparation time while improving the relevancy of your session. A content checklist simply lists the possibilities of your session. It's a rundown of the key points, possible examples, effective exercises, and pertinent anecdotes that you could include in your class. As you prepare you match the needs of the trainees to the relevant possibilities. This checklist is best kept on the computer or printed a few at a time because as you learn more about your subject and collect stories and examples from your participants, you'll want to add to your list.

Many people claim that checklists are a waste of time. I can't train without them. I also wouldn't get on a plane with a pilot who didn't use one!

Chris

Dear Unorganized:

As an aircraft owner, I'm really impressed that Chris is the one who used the example of a preflight checklist. It's amazing how easy it is to forget about things if we don't use a checklist! As you develop your people checklist, think about who they are, what you think they want, what their expectations are, and how you can best get your message across.

Check out the place where you'll have your program ahead of time. If that's impossible, get there early in case there are any last-minute changes that need to be made. More than once I've had to reset a room because of poor communication. If you're working with an off-site facility (hotel, community room, or social hall) it helps to send a diagram. Some room setups just don't translate well in conversation! Remember to ask if there are pillars or blind spots in the room. If it's a theater setting, will you be looking down at the group, or up at them? Perhaps you're getting the sense that there is little guarantee that you get what you want when it comes to the place, but a checklist can help ensure that you only experience a particular disaster once.

If you refer back to the section on the Trainer's Necessity Kit, your materials checklist will probably be at least half finished. It's nice to have everything you need once you get started. I like to use table cards for people's names and consistently forgot them until I put together a materials checklist. I like to carry extra writing paper for prolific participants, and always have a special take-home item for everyone. I even include a reminder to carry a map if my program is somewhere I haven't been before, and my client's phone number "just in case." You wouldn't want to know how often I've had to call home for that information, would you? Thanks for not asking!

Leslie

DEALING WITH THE LOGISTICS

All the world's a stage.

Shakespeare

If you enjoy the theater you can appreciate the effort it takes to construct the wonderful stage scenery that temporarily transports us to imaginary places that become so real as we watch the play. The efforts and ingenuity of these hardworking, behind-the-scenes stagehands makes it possible for us to enjoy special aspects of the production that have nothing to do with elocution or acting skills. We seldom have a grasp of how much work it takes to create these special places.

A training session is another setting where a special place is temporarily constructed; a place where people congregate to learn, explore, grow, and make decisions to change. And a training session, just like a theatrical production, requires a good deal of stage setting. You don't have a stage crew, and usually you don't have total control over what happens during your performance, yet you'll often be held responsible for what happens behind the scenes. If everything runs smoothly, you look like a star. If disaster strikes and you can't fix it, you look like an amateur.

As with other jobs well done, many aspects of a good training session are invisible. The better it goes, the fewer things you notice. If you've prepared your content and process, and if you take care of the "invisible" factors, you can stage a seamless production. There many factors to choreograph, but if you have an attractive, well-laid-out room, properly operating audiovisual equipment, sufficient materials for the size of the group, a varied and generous amount of refreshments, a comfortable temperature range, and an absence of interruptions or crises, all you really need to worry about is delivering the goods.

This section will give you a quick course on how to set yourself up for success in your training sessions. It will shorten your learning curve and help you avoid some of the unnecessary mistakes most people make when they become trainers. Tending to the logistics ahead of time will free you up to focus on the most important part of your training role: helping your learners succeed. When you do that well, everybody shines!

 Dear Instant Trainers:

I've been asked to present a workshop at our Regional Restaurant Association's annual meeting. They want me to share the way our restaurant has increased wine sales. The conference is in a town three states away. I want my workshop to be the talk of the conference, but I'm worried. How will I ever get all the logistics taken care of?

Distant in Dallas

Dear Distant:

This is no time to go it alone! There are people called *Meeting Planners* whose full-time job it is to make sure meetings run successfully. The first thing I would do is contact your association office. Ask them who on their staff is in charge of your meeting's logistics. Meeting planners provide a wealth of information. Here are a few questions they should be able to answer:

What is the profile of the people who will attend this meeting?

How many people are expected for this meeting?

How many people are expected to attend your session?

If you provide masters, will they reproduce your handouts?

What is the room you'll be presenting in like? (They may be able to provide a drawing of the room layout.)

What audiovisual equipment will be available?

Which audiovisual equipment works best in the room?

When will you be able to set up your materials?

How quickly will you have to be out of the room after your session?

With the answers to these questions, you can prepare a letter to the meeting planner describing the equipment, setup, and materials you'll need to have a successful program. Don't be surprised if while you're thinking about this, you get their checklist in the mail. They care just as much as you do that you have a successful session!

If your association is small and doesn't have anyone who fits this profile and your meeting is in a hotel, call their sales and catering department. Ask for the hotel's salesperson who's handling your meeting and ask her or him your logistical questions that deal with the room and equipment.

If neither of these ideas work in your situation, you could ask an associate who lives in the meeting area to go and look at the room for you. Your colleague's assessment will help you as you plan long-distance.

Distant, this is a time to create your own long-distance team. It just takes some creativity, a few phone calls, and a little luck!

Chris

Dear Distant:

You'll finish in first place if you cover the logistical details well in advance. Here are some items to add to your checklist. Make sure the room will be set up in the way that most meets your needs.

Will people need a place in which to mingle?

Is there a place in the room where you will want them to congregate?

Is your room off by itself or next to other meeting rooms?

What will be happening in other meeting rooms while your session is going on?

Where will you want the tables and chairs?

Is the entire room carpeted or is there a bare space for a dance floor?

How far away are the rest rooms?

If you have an idea of what you think will work well for your purposes, once you get the rough room size or dimensions, draw your ideas of how you want the room set up and send it to your contact person. You'll be amazed at the details that can be taken care of if you're willing to work closely with your contact person.

Leslie

Dear Instant Trainers:

I am preparing for my second presentation in a series of meetings on our new performance appraisal system for our hospital administrators. During our first meeting I realized that we have the ugliest training room in the world. We're talking pathetic! The walls are a very unattractive mud color, there are no windows in the room, and the carpet matches the walls. It's the only spot large enough to accommodate our group, so I have no choice as to where we meet. Any ideas on how to spruce up such an unattractive space when there's no budget for it?

Eyesore in El Paso

Dear Eyesore:

If you had some kind of budget, I'd suggest you purchase some wonderful motivational posters. The framed versions are pricey, but consider tacking or taping unframed posters to the wall. If you do purchase some posters, you're better off with "thematic" ones; that is, attractive photographs with very little text. Otherwise, people will want to read them during your session.

Here's a low-budget option: Go to a flea market or one of those dollar stores and see if you can find any framed photographs or prints for sale. Cheaper still, how about asking employees to go through their attics and donate an old picture or two?

If you look around your office you might find some brightly colored paper stock. You could create your own collection of quotations on your computer, run them through a laser printer, and make a series of mini-posters. The disadvantage of standard size sheets is that they can only be read close up, but the colors will still brighten up your room.

If you can get your hands on a flip chart (the oversized chart paper) and a few colored felt markers, you could write a series of quotations on the sheets and post them on the walls. Or find someone in your office who is artistic and enjoys the opportunity to get creative. The advantage to this last option is that you can easily replace your wall decorations with new ones. You can fold them, pack them away, and resurrect them at some point in the future. I hope these suggestions will help you "save the walls."

Leslie

Dear Eyesore:

If you're working with Leslie's flip chart suggestion, remember that you can create "bigger" posters by using the paper horizontally rather than vertically. Here's a neat trick I learned recently that requires no artistic talent (which made it usable for me): Take three or four different colored magic markers and rubber band them together. Use the bundled markers to draw a border around the edge of the flip chart sheet. This technique adds interest to anything you put on the rest of the paper.

Your low budget situation requires you to engage your creativity. Once you start looking for training room hang-ups, you'll be surprised at all the options you'll discover.

Chris

Dear Instant Trainers:

In our insurance company, we take turns leading weekly staff briefings and trainings because our business is constantly changing. Our training rooms are set up like standard classrooms; in fact, other than size, they all look disgustingly alike. As the coordinator of these meetings, I don't know if I should be concerned about our meeting site or not. Does room arrangement have any kind of impact on the trainer or participants and, if so, is there anything I can do with such limited resources?

Set Up in St. Petersburg

Dear Set Up:

Yes, room arrangement does make a difference and I'm sorry to hear your options are so limited. While standard classroom arrangement does focus everyone toward the front of the room, it is the least desirable setup for adult learners for several reasons. It limits the extent to which participants can communicate with each other, it conjures memories of negative experiences in schools, it limits people's ability to see each other, and it restricts physical movement.

Here are a couple of thoughts on improving the scheme of things, assuming that your budget prevents you from buying round tables. Could you turn your tables 180 degrees? This would allow participants to sit on both sides of the tables so they could face each other. If your training sessions require discussion, you have instantly improved the conditions for interaction.

Another option is the herringbone arrangement, which is a variation of the standard classroom. Simply push the outside corner of the outside tables toward the front of the room 45 degrees, leaving the middle row as is. It would look something like an amphitheater setup. I hope these suggestions perk up your room a bit so you will feel less "set up."

Leslie

Dear Set Up:

When it comes to training room setup, I hate straight lines. Can you change into jeans and a sweatshirt one afternoon? If so, do a quick change, push up your sleeves, and go to work as a furniture mover. Try several different arrangements of your tables and chairs. After each move, try sitting in various seats around the room. Check for three things: Do you you have an unobstructed view of where any audiovisual equipment will be set up? Can you see where the presenter will be? And, will you be able to see the other participants? After trying a few arrangements, choose the one that works the best from all three perspectives.

Chris

 Dear Instant Trainers:

I am a new teller trainer in a small credit union. I am not a maintenance engineer, logistics specialist, nor a supreme being capable of controlling erratic temperatures and distractions. Yet I've discovered that my trainees hold me responsible for room conditions and I'm the one who takes the heat when things go wrong. How can I cope with this?

Taking the Heat in Hot Springs

Dear Taking the Heat:

Every trainer has horror stories about soaring temperatures or freezing rooms, emergencies, fire alarms, noise, distractions, interruptions, and other logistical nightmares. Yes, it is unfortunate that trainers must assume responsibility for everything that happens in their classrooms, including conditions beyond their control. Here are a few suggestions for coping with these challenges:

If you spot a potential problem it often helps to acknowledge it early on in your session to lessen the irritation factor. Explain the situation without excessive apology to avoid hinting that you are responsible for everything. Perhaps you will be buoyed by what I call the "shipwreck theory." I think that discomfort experienced by a group can serve as a bonding factor. It can even enhance your presentation, if it's handled with a sense of humor.

Let participants observe your efforts to help them be as comfortable as possible. They'll be impressed. A special thank you for their flexibility also helps. In short, you cannot control external circumstances, but you can control how you react to them. Your expression of concern for comfort (despite your inability to do anything about it) and your example of flexibility could be the best lessons trainees take away from your sessions.

Leslie

Dear Taking the Heat:

I remember doing a program for a group of women in a hotel meeting room. The front half of the room was freezing and the back half was boiling. As the hotel worked to adjust things, I dubbed the front of the room the menopause section and the back half the premenopause section. Everyone laughed and the women got up and moved according to their current hormonal activity. A sense of humor really helps!

Chris

 Dear Instant Trainers:

My boss has asked me to coordinate our annual All Staff Meeting (annual report, staff awards, and organizational rally) and we are holding it at the local country club. We will be meeting in a wonderful room with one wall that is all windows, overlooking a spectacular view. The person at the country club suggested we put our lectern in front of the window, so staff can take in this wonderful view during our meeting. Is this a good idea?

Scenic in Santa Fe

Dear Scenic:

What an insightful question! I would discourage you from this particular setup because if the view is stunning, it could detract from whomever is presenting. In addition, you'll be setting up what is called a backlight condition, which means everyone will be looking into a bright natural light source. The face of anyone standing in front of the window will be difficult for the audience to see. What's more, your meeting could give everyone a headache! Not because of what they hear, but because of what they see. Backlighting creates eyestrain; when people gaze at bright light for an extended period they often end up with a pounding head. You might want to give yourself a break: Turn the room around and let everyone enjoy the spectacular view during breaks.

Leslie

Dear Scenic:

The Instant Trainers don't always agree and this is one of those times. I favor using the outside view as a backdrop. Find out what direction the windows face so you can determine where the sun will be during your meeting. If it is a northern or southern exposure you won't have to worry about the light unless you're using slides or overheads. I'm one of those people who think that although a view might be momentarily distracting, most people find looking at nature as a healthy, pleasant pause. As long as you're not dealing with the morning sun from the east or afternoon glare from the west, I'd use the window and the view as an added bonus for the meeting.

Chris

 Dear Instant Trainers:

In the course of my professional life I have sat in on more dry, drawn out training meetings than is humane. As a new leader of volunteers in our human services agency, I could unknowingly inflict comparable punishment on my trainees, but I want to take a kinder and gentler approach. What are the "rules" about providing refreshments and taking breaks and just how long can people sit before they want to take it out on the trainer?

Concerned in Cleveland

Dear Concerned:

In the past, as a trainee, maybe you've suffered from hunger, thirst, inappropriate temperature, or a bursting bladder and wished the trainer had called a time out. Yes, breaks and refreshments add a comfort factor to training. People enjoy having something to drink and munch on. Some people call it "feed and lead."

If you offer liquid refreshments, please remember that not all people are coffee drinkers. It's nice to offer a variety of caffeinated and decaffeinated drinks (hot and cold). Some people like diet sodas; some don't. Where refreshments are concerned, just a little bit of effort on your part can make you look good and your trainees feel good.

You asked about breaks? Breaks are important. It's nice to have a formal break at least every 90 minutes. Most of us are pretty active in our jobs; few of us sit for hours at a time. We like to move, mingle, and enjoy a bit of structured distraction. If you mingle too, and listen closely, you'll find that some important discussions often take place during breaks. Besides giving your trainees a break, it's important for you, too. An incidental comment made during break time can give you just the real-life example you needed, or help you adjust your emphasis so you can better meet the needs of your trainees. So relax, kick back, and give yourself (and everyone else) a break— you deserve it!

Leslie

Dear Concerned:

One of the biggest lessons I learned about being a compassionate trainer came from being a student. While I was attending a class it occurred to me that I needed many more breaks to go to the bathroom than I did when presenting. It dawned on me that the difference was water. As a participant, with those pitchers of water sitting on the table in front of me, I was consuming much more liquid than when presenting. I learned that as a trainer, using myself as a guide for calling breaks wasn't such a good idea. So, in presenting your material, if you're tempted to stretch things for a few more minutes before calling the break, take a look at the empty water pitchers sitting on each table and remember how hard it is to learn when you're thinking about your need for a rest room!

Chris

Dear Instant Trainers:

The first time I presented information to our School Improvement Team, the maintenance staff began mowing the lawn just outside our room and we could hardly hear each other. A group of parents walked in, thinking our room was where they were supposed to meet. The overhead projector light burned out; the telephone rang so many times we ended up unplugging it. I was as burned out as the overhead bulb by the time I finished. What's the best way to handle crises and inconveniences such as this?

Frazzled in Frankfort

Dear Frazzled:

It may lend you little comfort to know that Murphy's Law usually presides over meetings and educational institutions are not exempt. Perhaps the little known "O'Toole's Law" might help put it in perspective: O'Toole's Law states that Murphy was an optimist! Yes, it helps to take things in stride.

Despite the reality that things will go wrong, there are two strategies to help you prevail: 1) prevention, and 2) flexibility. Preventive measures involve controlling your environment as much as possible. For example, if you'll be using an overhead or slide projector, know ahead of time how to use it and how to do routine maintenance such as replacing bulbs. Carry with you, or request, an extra bulb.

Carry an extension cord, too, just in case. Put a "Meeting in Progress" sign on the door indicating that you don't want to be interrupted. You can even list where other meetings are being held at the same time in the same building so no one will open your door. You can't control noisy activities such as lawn mowing, construction projects, and equipment being moved or installed. One option might require a brief interruption, such as finding out if any other area (preferably far away) could be mowed or worked on until your meeting is over.

It doesn't help to blame the noisy people; after all, they're just doing their jobs, too. A little tact and flexibility on your part can go a long way. You can't control it all. If prevention fails you, opt for flexibility and let the shipwreck theory prevail. Share the disaster with your group as goodheartedly as you can. Maybe these strategies will help you and your colleagues prevail in spite of it all.

Leslie

Dear Frazzled:

At least the marching band wasn't practicing! Leslie's right. Prepare for all the disasters you can possibly imagine and think through what you'll do if they actually happen. Having a Plan B is a good idea for training situations as well as life. When even Plan B, C, or D won't work, your only option is to roll with the situation. I've seen trainers lose their group, not because they couldn't fix a problem, but because they let the problem become more important than the learning. Keep your cool and the participants will keep theirs.

Chris

 ### Dear Instant Trainers:

I've been subjected to some taxing training situations where presenters seemed totally clueless that their audience had long since "hit the wall." The trainer seemed to be having a good time of it, but as students, we were desperate for a break, group activity, or some other kind of humane intervention. I don't want my programs to end up on the FDA list of new forms of anesthesia. How can I protect my audience from a similar fate?

Concerned in Cleveland

Dear Concerned:

Regardless of how interesting your lecture is or how compelling your program, physical fatigue is one of the many challenges you face. Whether your sessions last half a day (three to four hours) or a full day (six to eight hours), physical and mental fatigue will be factors. Most working adults experience some level of physical activity in their jobs; they walk around, engage in a variety of tasks, and freely move about. That's what they're used to, but in a training program they just sit.

The conventional wisdom used to be that people should not sit in the same position for more than 45 minutes at a time. These days, we're told that people's attention spans are short (think of watching television with a remote in your hand) and that every 20 minutes there should be some kind of shift in format. If your sessions tend to run an entire day or even half a day, this means you want activities that involve physical movement and mental involvement at least twice in the morning and twice in the afternoon, in addition to your scheduled refreshment breaks.

You can have people stand up for a moment, move them into groups, have them work on projects, role plays, hands-on, or other involving activities. You'll find more on activities and exercises in Appendix B.

There are early warning signs of fatigue. Note people's posture. Normally, when people are alert they sit straight or lean forward with a look of interest on their faces. When fatigue sets in, eye contact is replaced with unfocused stares. Response time increases, too. Are there long pauses after you ask a question, accompanied by little or no eye contact? Either your group is zoned out or you've asked a very difficult (or unclear) question. If people seem cooperative but confused, it could be fatigue. Get them up, ask them to talk with each other, or stand up and do a quick stretch.

Fatigue can create listless behavior and it can also create restlessness. Some people will sit very still while others will fidget. If people are constantly adjusting their positions, chances are they are fatigued. Tired groups don't tend to laugh as much as alert groups. If some of your proven, never-fail witty remarks and humorous stories barely get a smile, your group may need a break. Give them one.

If you see people making side glances or comments to each other, this may be a sign that they are bored or tired. Be an optimist. Assume they're tired. Participants appreciate a trainer's sensitivity to their needs. Fatigue is inevitable; expect it, look for it, try to prevent it, and respond to it when you see it. Your group will appreciate your efforts, and now you have a few options for keeping everyone alert and awake.

Leslie

Dear Concerned:

Did you think Leslie covered everything, or did you figure I'd have one more thing to add? Well, I do. One of my favorite fatigue fighters is, weather permitting, to send a class outside during a break. If we're meeting in a place familiar to the participants, I'll ask them to go outside and look for something they've never noticed before. If they're in a new environment, I'll ask that they go outside and look for something interesting. After the break I'll ask a few people to share what they've discovered and ask how it felt to breathe some fresh air. You'll be surprised at what people observe and how good it feels for them to reconnect with the world outside of the classroom.

Chris

IDENTIFYING AND ORGANIZING MATERIAL

If you don't know where you're going, any road will take you there!

Alice In Wonderland

Those were Alice's words during her adventures in Wonderland. This philosophy seemed okay for her, but you'll have unhappy trainees if you can't help them see where this training session is taking them. While the ability to live with uncertainty is a critical skill as we face the future, it doesn't do much to enhance learning.

Adults are silently asking for connections during a training session. They want to know how what they're learning connects with what they already know. They want to know how your material connects with what they'll be doing in the future. They want to know how these ideas will make their lives easier, better, or simpler. They want you, the trainer, to tell them. And they would like you to explain this right away so they can decide whether or not the time spent in this session will be worth their attention.

Just a quick word on forced attendance. Mandatory sessions only guarantee that bodies show up. You're the one who has to work on getting the participants to engage their brains for learning and their hearts for caring.

Training is like an iceberg, most of it below the surface, unnoticed until, of course, someone runs into it and by that time it's too late—the boat is sinking. The time you spend finding, choosing, and organizing your material won't be obvious to the people in your session. The time you **don't** spend will be noticeable! A lot of training preparation is like this: invisible to the participant unless it's not there.

This section will help you make some important decisions. You'll get advice on how to start and how to end. You'll receive insights on what to put in the middle. You'll find a formula for giving clear instructions. Your time will be well spent.

Dear Instant Trainers:

I work in a small dental practice and we pride ourselves on keeping up our skills in dentistry trends and practices. The partners in our office have encouraged us to initiate a "Lunch 'n Learn" program series for the Dental Assistants and Hygienists. We will discuss journal articles and exchange what we know about the most current dental practice literature. I've been asked to organize it and lead the first few meetings, although I've never done anything like this before. I don't even know where to begin. The one thing I know is, we want to keep it sweet and simple because I don't have a lot of extra time to prepare for this kind of thing. Where do I begin?

Learning in Latrobe

Dear Learning:

You're probably further along than you think, because I suspect you already have a list of the journals that feature the kinds of articles you're looking for. I also figure you're aware of the trends and current practices that have the most potential for affecting your practice or your patients. At any rate, these would be your first two steps. As for organizing the Lunch 'n Learn sessions and keeping them simple, I'm happy to help. I'd suggest you lead the first few sessions, and then rotate the responsibility. If you do a good job, everyone who follows can profit from your good example. Each of you has a different style and approach, and the variety will be great.

To make your Lunch 'n Learn sessions successful, you need to agree on a time, place, and length of session (45 minutes is ideal). Everyone will need a copy of the article to discuss and, of course, they need to read it prior to the meeting.

As a group leader, the best way to cover your assigned topics is to create a series of substantive questions that will encourage discussion, comparisons, and opinions. Here are some examples:

What did the author say about…?

What was your reaction…?

How does this compare to your (our) experience…?

How does this relate to us (our practice) (our patients)…?

How will this affect our field?

How will this affect us (our practice) (our patients)…?

What do we need to do with this information…?

What else do we need to know…?

Once you establish a standard set of questions, use them as a template from meeting to meeting. Group leaders can vary the wording as they see fit. Ask your coworkers to share the responsibility for discussion, and your Lunch 'n Learn series is off and running. I hope these suggestions give you plenty of food for thought.

Leslie

Dear Learning:

In the movie, The Graduate, *Dustin Hoffman's character was told that the word* **"plastics"** *was the key to success. I have a word for you—food. As you plan your Lunch 'n Learn, consider the power of a healthy dessert. If your promotional flyers and conversations promise a goodie to liven up everyone's brown-bag lunches, you'll increase interest and possibly attendance. There are many low-fat, low-sugar bars and cookies available and fresh fruit is always a good choice. There's something about people getting together for a treat that helps the conversation flow.*

Chris

Dear Instant Trainers:

Our medical practice has just purchased its first computers and I get to be the resident expert on our systems. They sent me off for training and now there's an expectation that I can teach everyone in our office every-thing I learned. Well, this is great in theory but I've never done a training session before, let alone anything so technical. I don't even know how much I learned. There's got to be a way to get my material organized but I'm not sure where to start. What approach should I use and how will I know if I'm actually teaching anyone anything? Please help!

Bowled Over in Bowling Green

Dear Bowled Over:

Yes, it is a lofty task that lies ahead of you, but help is here. Let's assume you will first give a brief orientation on the software to your office team. To help you get organized I suggest you cover a few simple but essen-tial learning points, such as:

> **What** the software is designed to do;
>
> **Why** the practice chose this software over other products;
>
> **Who** will be working on the system;
>
> **How** it generally works and the benefits of converting to this technology.

If you wanted or needed to, you could throw in a **when.** That is, when you (or the practice partners) expect everything to be up and running, though time lines are often less than dependable. Considering that you will continue normal office hours during the conversion, you'll need to be flexi-ble in this area.

Now that we've organized the flow of material for your orientation, let's move on to the one-on-one aspect of training. You first need to deter-mine what each staff member knows about computers. Pay attention to how they feel about this change too; attitudes about learning a new system may range from anxiety and nervousness to excitement and eagerness. Be will-ing to take whatever you get. Make sure you've practiced the basic steps beforehand so you can comfortably demonstrate the essentials. Here are the steps to follow for technical training:

1. **Describe the process.** Your explanation may involve a quick review of what you covered in your orientation. Try to keep it simple and organized. Avoid extraneous information. Watch the person's face for indicators of interest, absorption of your instructions, or confusion. Of course, if you detect confusion, stop and clarify issues with the person before moving on.

2. **Demonstrate it.** Show the trainee how it's done. Once may not be enough. Watch the person closely to determine how well he or she is doing. Be patient and encouraging. Answer questions as simply as possible and repeat yourself when necessary.

3. **Discuss the process.** Once you've demonstrated the first steps stop and ask if there are any questions. If you sense nervousness or resistance on the part of the trainee, let the person know this is to be expected. If you've had any humorous experiences (or know of anyone who has), this is the perfect time to inject a bit of levity. And if you sense the person has a question but won't ask it, offer a quick review.

4. **Drill.** Let the trainee try it. Monitor the process and offer encouragement and more explanation if it's needed. Let your trainee go through the steps more than one time to be sure he or she has them down. Ask the person to describe the process step by step so you can check the absorption of what you've covered so far.

5. **Discuss.** Talk about what the trainee did, the whats and whys of the process and answer any questions he or she may have. Add additional bits of information if you think the person has a good grasp of what you've covered.

6. **Determine** if it's time to review and repeat, or to move on to another step. Follow this process with each person and your training should be successful. This approach keeps you one or two steps ahead of your trainees (a process many graduate students and college instructors use when teaching a new class). You can go back to your manual, review the next step in the process, practice it, and then teach it to someone else. As with anything else, just take one step at a time.

Leslie

Dear Bowled Over:

Here are a few more words on the topic of the learner actually practicing the new skill. If there is one area where training programs fail, this is it. When time is an issue, it's easy for both the trainer and the learner to agree to let the practice go. The trainer says, "You've got it, right?" and the learner responds with, "Sure, no problem." Both are relieved. The trainer doesn't have to worry about answering hard questions and the learner doesn't have to prove mastery of the new process. This is not training! When you plan your sessions, make sure you have plenty of time for hands-on practice. You'll be a better trainer and your students will have learned a whole lot more.

Chris

Dear Instant Trainers:

I've seen a lot of trainers in my time, some of them good and some of them not so good. Now that I will be a trainer, I want to do it right, or at least as right as I can. I'm a stickler for detail and some of my worst moments as a trainee have been when the trainer seemed disorganized or lost us while presenting a list of strategies, tips, or suggestions. How can I avoid those pitfalls?

Organized in Ogden

Dear Organized:

There could probably be a lengthy answer to your question, but I'll give you the short one instead. The secret is in consistency. The mistake some trainers make is deviating from whatever system they are using. If you say, "Point number one ..." make sure you follow with a two, three, and subsequent numbers. If you start out with roman numerals, use them throughout the sequence.

Don't you hate it when the trainer gives you five points and you end up with seven? Well, there are ways to prevent this! When explaining a series of points in your lecture bits, do your best to keep each item separate from the others. Let participants know when you're moving on; many trainers don't make it clear when they have ended one item and moved on to another. Keep this in mind and your participants will end up with the same number of items on their lists as you!

Leslie

Dear Organized:

One more way to be organized is to print up a flip chart, overhead transparency, or handout with your important points. In fact, for key learning points, I'd do all three. I'd use an overhead to keep myself on track. (If you have several points to cover, place a sheet under your transparency and expose one item at a time. Read about the "Revelation" technique in Chapter 20 for more details.) I'd pass out a "fill in the blank" handout listing the key points with a few words missing so participants will take notes. And when I finished the section, I'd put up a flip chart summarizing the points so they'd be visible during the rest of the class. These techniques will help you stay on track and enhance the learning experience.

Chris

Dear Instant Trainers:

Help! I work in a large dental office and recently the practice partners decided they wanted to improve our customer service. I'm complimented they put me in charge of this project, but I don't know what I'm doing. My assignment is to teach service skills to our office staff. How will I know what to teach? How does a person go about selecting the right material for customer service (or any other kind of) training?

Desperate in Duluth

Dear Desperate:

Your dilemma will actually come from too many choices rather than too few unless you focus. Here are some questions to help you zero in on specifics:

- Who is the audience: Reception? Assistants? Hygienists? Schedulers? Bookkeepers?
- What do you want to emphasize: Telephone skills? Face-to-face service with patients or clients? With vendors?
- Is internal service (teamwork) a consideration?

- Are there are any current problem areas in your internal systems or patient delivery systems?

- Are you easy and convenient to deal with: making appointments, rescheduling, offering reasonable waiting periods, billing, and follow-up?

- What kind of feedback are you receiving from patients (both compliments and criticism)?

Patient complaints are a great source for potential training topics, as are complaints from office staff. Note all of the areas you and everyone else identify as problematic. Once you've begun answering these questions you can go to any good bookstore and find books on the particular area of service you want or need to focus on. By the way, avoid the common mistake of trying to teach everything in one session. Just think of your sessions as intense discussions and you'll feel more capable. Pick the areas that reflect the greatest need and focus your energies there first. Please remember that you know more about this subject than you think. If you take one step at a time you'll be amazed at how quickly it all falls into place.

Leslie

Dear Desperate:

Before you have a heart attack, keep reading. Check out Appendix C and look for the name and address of Crisp Publications. They carry a wonderful list of helpful workbooks that can be a foundation for training sessions in many subject areas. The format might be just what you're looking for: brief treatments of work-related topics with questions, exercises, and activities. You can use them as workbooks for your program or as a starting point for a session you customize. They are well written (many of them by friends of the Instant Trainers), illustrated, and affordable.

Chris

 Dear Instant Trainers:

Now that I'm a trainer, I want to do a good job at it. The last training session I attended was a disaster because the person conducting the training had obviously never been trained on how to give instructions effectively. In our small group, half the time we just did what we wanted because we weren't clear on what was expected of us. Now, this may be an impossible question for you to answer, but is there any kind of "formula" one could use for giving clear instructions?

Directionless in Detroit

Dear Directionless:

Put it in writing. Here's what I mean: Most trainers have a clear idea of what they want to have happen in a small group activity. So they give a quick explanation and wait. The group waits, too. For more instructions, that is. Remember the old GIGO (garbage in, garbage out) from the days when computers were new? Well, the same principle applies to an adult learning environment. If you can express the outcome you want or expect, in two to four short steps, chances are you'll get it.

Write the steps on a transparency or flip chart so everyone can see them during the entire exercise. Watch how often someone looks up to check the next step. If you have one last step that is different from the others, or you want to build up to a grand finale, save that last step (don't show it) until the others have been covered. This helps direct your group's attention where you want it.

Leslie

Dear Directionless:

Flip chart or not, there will always be some people who won't follow directions no matter how clear you make them! These are the same people who put things together from the picture on the box rather than the text in the instructions, so make sure you give them a picture. In training, the picture is a clear description of the desired final product. As you give your step-by-step instructions on one flip chart, display another that describes what you expect people to have accomplished by the end of the exercise.

Chris

 Dear Instant Trainers:

When someone was teaching me about sales, I remember them saying, "People remember first things." If that's true about training also, openings must be important. Can you give me any tips on how to get a training session off to a good start?

Opening in Orlando

Dear Opening:

Think "Lights, camera, action!" and "On your mark, get set, go!" Listen again to the sounds of the orchestra at the start of your favorite musical. Remember the opening scene of the best movie you ever saw. Reread the opening lines of your most cherished book. One way or another, they all have something in common—they captured your attention and excited you about what was coming next. That's what the opening of a training session should do, too!

I can't tell you how many training programs I've attended that started like this:

> *"Good morning."*
> (Trainer pauses for response and then says in a louder voice)
> *"Good Morning."*
> (Trainer waits for bigger response from the participants.)
> *"That's better. Before we get started this morning I'd like to fill you in on a few housekeeping details. The bathrooms are down the hall, we will have a break at 10:00 A.M...."*

Do you think Spielberg would accept a script that started like that? I doubt it. Every time I hear this or a variation of this pattern, I assume I'm in for a long day. Yes, the housekeeping stuff is important, but it's not the most important. If the research is accurate, and you have less than seven seconds to give people the information (verbal and nonverbal) that they will use to judge you, this opening won't get you off to the start you want.

I've had the opportunity to watch one of my idols, Bette Midler, perform live several times. Here's what I've learned from watching her that I've translated into an effective opening sequence for my sessions. I figure, if it works for her on stage, night after night, it can work for me in the training room!

There are three parts to a good opening sequence:

1. Be done with your preparations at least 15 minutes before the session starts and spend those 15 minutes meeting and talking to participants as the arrive. Bette's not shaking hands with the masses as they enter the auditorium, but her presence is there. You can buy a program or a T-shirt and all the staff are wearing something and projecting an attitude that reminds you that Bette's going to be on stage soon—just for you.

2. Make the first thing you say connect immediately to the participant's need. If you do that, you send a strong message to all participants that they're going to get value for the time they're investing. Every time I've seen the Divine Miss M perform, she's started with one of her most famous songs, one we were dying to hear. We knew right away we were going to get our money's worth.

3. After you've connected with the audience's need for the subject, connect yourself to the audience. Someone wise once said, "People don't care how much you know till they know how much you care." After her first song, Bette chats with the audience, but not the kind of chat that comes directly out of a city guide book or memorizing a few lines written by a publicist. She says things that let you know that she's gotten to know your area.

I predict if you work on your opening, both you and your class will get more out of your training session.

Chris

Dear Opening:

At the risk of sounding compulsive, I'd suggest you be there at least a half hour before beginning. For my taste, 15 minutes is cutting it way too short. In extending the "Lights, camera, action!" metaphor, think about clever ways you can establish your presence even if you have to leave the room while your learners are filing in. Think of Chris sitting in that dark theater, expectantly waiting for the Divine Miss M to appear. There's a magical presence in that theater before her feet hit the stage.

For a trainer, maybe it's the materials lying neatly on the tables. Or that friendly "Welcome to this session" note on the flip chart or whiteboard. Maybe it's that cartoon on the overhead projector, or those intriguing little toys on the head table. Or those Tootsie Rolls. Or those flip chart sheets on the wall that have obviously just been put up, but that are folded and taped up so you can't see what they say yet.

You get the drift. There are clever or subtle ways you can create positive anticipation of your presence so people have a sense of you even before you begin. We can't all be a Bette Midler or a Robin Williams, but we can capture that sense of the special every time!

Leslie

Dear Instant Trainers:

I've gotten in the habit of spending a few quiet minutes each evening to collect my thoughts from all that went on during the day—looking for insights and things to put on my to-do list. This exercise gives me a nice sense of closure for the day. As I was doing it yesterday, it occurred to me that training sessions probably need a well-thought-out ending. What should the end of a training session be like?

Finished in Phoenix

Dear Finished:

I always think of closings as the time when you help people understand what to do with what they've learned. The underlying purpose of training is always some form of change—new skills, different behaviors, or an improved attitude. The question you have to ask yourself is, "Do the people in my session know what's expected of them when the program is over?" Too often, I'm afraid, the answer is no. Your job is to make the expected action clear.

Here's a simple exercise I use quite often to help people understand that learning isn't only what happens in the classroom, but what happens when everyone goes back to the real world. This exercise, followed by a few well-chosen, inspirational words, makes a great ending.

> *Step One:* Ask all participants to take out business cards or put their names and phone numbers on index cards that you provide.
>
> *Step Two:* Ask them to write the date you've chosen (a workday 15 to 30 days after your session) on the front of the cards.
>
> *Step Three:* Ask the participants to write on the back of the card one or two things that they intend to do differently, practice further, or learn more about as a result of your class.
>
> *Step Four:* Have each participant exchange a card with someone else. (Preferably this should be someone they do not know well or work closely with on a daily basis.) Explain that the pair should call each other on the date you've selected to check in and determine how well they're doing with their commitments.

Since no training course, however long, can replace the need for trying new skills, behaviors, and attitudes in the actual work environment, your ending needs to challenge people to take that responsibility on for themselves.

Chris

Dear Finished:

People often complain that no matter how motivated they feel at the end of a session, that motivation just doesn't last. I remind them that a good meal doesn't last either, but we find a way to feed ourselves again, don't we? I think of my training sessions as plenty of food for thought, and I like to serve dessert.

Here's how I do it: I bring along a pile of envelopes that just happens to match the number of people attending my session. At the end of the program I ask them to fill out a special action sheet I've designed (usually the last page of their workbook), outlining what they learned and how they plan to apply the information. If there's no workbook I may bring postcards and ask everyone to write down something they plan to take action on, or do differently. I ask the participants to self-address the envelopes, stuff them with the forms they've filled out, and seal them. I collect them, take them with me, and mail them out two or three weeks later. I follow the same routine with the postcards, adding the reminder that other people might read them, and suggesting that people refrain from writing anything too personal on the postcards. Participants tell me they really enjoy getting their own words back, and it serves as a reminder that what is learned in the classroom can be transferred into everyday life.

In case you're wondering, I pay for the stamps. It seems a small price to pay for the satisfaction of knowing I've added a sweet ending to a delightful day of learning.

Leslie

 Dear Instant Trainers:

I don't know anything about training, but thanks to our organization's downsizing I need to learn quickly! My only real frame of reference is school. Am I supposed to give people homework?

Assigned in Albany

Dear Assigned:

It's easy to think "school" when you are asked to do training. My first bit of advice is to remember the very best experiences you had in the classroom. Sometimes we unconsciously remember and mimic both the good and the bad!

But your question was about homework. I'd suggest, unless your session is divided into several parts, you might want to consider prework instead. Prework is material or an assignment you send out to students before the session. Its purpose is to bring people to class already having thought about or gotten insights into the subject you'll be covering. Here are a few examples to illustrate what I mean.

- An article reprint that deals with your subject.
- An assignment for participants (with specific questions included) to interview two customers before a customer service training session.
- A series of questions for participants to answer about a recent feedback experience for a session on performance reviews.

The real key with a prework assignment is that it must tie in closely with your subject and you must work it into your session so that people don't feel as though they've been given busywork to do. The real value of a prework assignment is that it gives participants the opportunity to have one piece of knowledge in common as they start learning together.

Chris

Dear Assigned:

Maybe I'm a cynic, but while I love the concept, I've had some difficulties with preprogram work assignments. I've also found that if you're clever or incredibly persistent, you can create interest on the part of your learners. So my first thought is to give it a try. See what kind of response you get and if you think it's worth it. Here are a couple of issues and how to work around them.

Avoid making the preprogram assignment a prerequisite. This is because you won't get 100 percent compliance, so you'll have to cover some of that information anyway. So make it sort of an added-value experience. As for combating apathy, you could try creating team competitions. You could give out individual or team prizes for those who complete their assignments.

You could also use the preprogram work as a nice icebreaker, asking people to compare their own projects with someone else's, thus opening your session with a spirited exchange. So I guess I'm not completely cynical about this, but you have to be clear on what you are doing and why. Good luck with your assignments, and if you run into some clever strategies to help get people to respond, please keep your Instant Trainers in the loop.

Leslie

Dear Instant Trainers:

I work in the order-taking department of a small plastics firm. The materials for the training session on listening I've been asked to lead look pretty good. It's good, it's just not mine. I'd like to personalize the material with some of my own stuff. The problem is, I don't have my own stuff! Where can I find material that I can use?

Looking in Lexington

Dear Looking:

Material that personalizes a program really enhances learning. Most people don't realize that life provides material on a daily basis. I find material in three places: my experiences, other people's experiences (what Cavett Robert calls OPE), and the media. You should be looking in all three.

Going to the library once a month to browse through the magazines, reading a daily newspaper, watching movies, and reading books will provide you with an endless stream of examples and stories to liven up your sessions.

Listening to other people's stories (even asking for them: "What's the worst listening behavior you've ever observed and how did it make you feel?") will eventually provide a great example you can use. Often other people's experiences will come to light during a training session. Take a few notes at the break so you won't forget them and ask the participants for permission to use the stories in other sessions. (You can promise to change the names or alter a few details if necessary.)

Don't overlook the experiences you've had or will have. One of the bonuses of doing training is that even when things are going badly, you may be able to turn the experience into a story you can use later.

You may want to read the questions and answers in Chapter 15, Delivering Your Content. The answer on storytelling might be particularly helpful when you find something you want to turn into material for your session.

Chris

Dear Looking:

I'm a little embarrassed to bring this up, but there's a gold mine of great stories, memorable examples, and humorous illustrations in old Reader's Digests. *I mean **old**. Don't use recent issues because many of your audience members may have just read them. But go back five or ten years and you'll find some clever items that sound new because everyone has forgotten them. Of course, this means you're going for the classical rather than topical examples, and those are the best. I discovered this years ago while spending three nights in a little motel in Wheatland, Wyoming when I perused three old* Reader's Digests *with great passion because this was the only reading material I could find. I still remember a couple of the illustrations, and every now and then I still use them.*

Another fun way to collect stories is to ask people to relate their most embarrassing moments. Or listen to children who are ten years old or younger. I've begun asking anyone I meet what their jobs are like and how people treat them. I'm building a whole new repertoire!

Leslie

FACILITATING THE LEARNING PROCESS

Smart people don't have all the answers; they're the ones with the best questions.

I'm not certain where or when it started, but at some point people started believing that having the answer to any question was a sign of greater intelligence than having a good question was. We'd like to change this commonly held notion. The smartest people we've encountered over the years have often remarked that the more they delved into their subject of choice, whether it was management, a leisure pursuit, or computer programming, the more they realized they didn't know!

Making the learning process work for all participants isn't a matter of giving them a list of questions with the corresponding answers. It's an opportunity to help them find the questions that are meaningful to them and their circumstances. Trainers who understand this are concerned with their ability to facilitate learning, not hung up on coming to class with all the right answers.

A colleague trainer, Roxanne Emmerich, told me about a professor she had in college. He spent the entire semester facing the chalkboard, writing equations, and talking, as it seemed to the students, to himself. On the last day of class, the day before exams, he put down the chalk, turned to the class, and said, "Does anyone have any questions?"

Extreme? Yes, but unfortunately each of us has been in a similar situation. During the last five minutes of the session, the trainer says, "Does anyone have any questions?" No one responds and the trainer says "I guess I must have explained it all very well." To quote the popular game, Balderdash!

There is no greater art form that a trainer can master than the ability to invite participants to ask questions comfortably and then to respond to those questions effectively. Read on; you'll get some great ideas that will make you really smart.

Dear Instant Trainers:

The last session I did on meeting management felt confusing to me and I was leading it! Our discussions seemed to jump back and forth and by the time the session was over, I was convinced that no one learned very much. Is there a right order for material that helps learners learn? I don't want to do it that way again.

Out of Order in Ottawa

Dear Out of Order:

You've just stumbled on the concept of sequencing training. Knowing the term isn't important, but understanding the meaning is. Think of a baby's development. First she learns how to hold her head up, then roll over, then sit up, then crawl, then stand up, and finally walk. Each skill builds on the one learned before. Learning during a training session is no different.

When you're doing technical training, it's pretty easy to see the pattern. There is an obvious sequence to the material and you have to master one concept before moving on to the next. Other training (often referred to as soft skills training) is a little trickier.

Your assignment on meeting management, for example, has identifiable parts but no mandatory sequence. You'll have to determine a way to connect the parts that makes it easier for the learner to comprehend and remember. The most common patterns that work well have to do with time. Here are a few examples: before, during, and after (works well for your meeting management session); yesterday, today, and tomorrow (works well for an employee orientation); or beginning, middle, and end (works well when dealing with change).

Spending time thinking about the sequence of your material will pay off in ease of delivery and increased learning!

Chris

Dear Out of Order:

If we haven't honed our topic, sometimes it feels as if we're circling the field rather than landing. If your topic is meeting management, it would be helpful for you to scan some of your trade magazines to clarify your personal approach to the process. It might be helpful to ask yourself some questions before you conduct another session.

> *How do you define meeting management?*
>
> *What do you think is most important in teaching someone else this topic?*
>
> *What are the biggest mistakes people typically make and how can you avoid them?*
>
> *What were some of your biggest mistakes and will they make good examples?*
>
> *What is essential information for your learners?*
>
> *What falls into the category of "nice to know?"*
>
> *What kinds of stories or illustrations do you have to help make your key points?*
>
> *After reading Chris's sequence choices, which will work best for you?*

Having the information is one thing; being able to present it in a coherent fashion is another. So, Out of Order, don't be discouraged; sometimes it takes a while to get organized. Just spend a few minutes pondering these points, and I think things will fall into place for you!

Leslie

Dear Instant Trainers:

I know leading a training session isn't the same as teaching school, but the other day I got to remembering how my spelling grades improved in the third grade. I always did better on the Friday test after Mrs. Paris started Thursday reviews. I never thought of reviewing during a training session, I guess because I don't have a test. But maybe I'm not doing as good a job for my participants as Mrs. Paris did for me. Any suggestions?

Reviewless in Redondo

Dear Reviewless:

Your question is a great example of a the value of a walk down memory lane. Mrs. Paris was a great teacher because she understood that repetition increases retention. The difference between her class and yours is in how you refer to your review.

Most adults will give you a funny look if you pause and say, "Let's stop for a few minutes and review what we've covered." They think that you're insulting their intelligence because they're beyond the need for reviews. No one is beyond review. A good review enhances the learning of the most intelligent people. Who knows, maybe it's the reviews that make them so intelligent; it worked for spelling! So, your job is to make a review not **feel** like a review! Here are two ideas.

- Read the questions in Chapter 21, Putting Fun in Your Training, to learn a little about training games. A game is a great way to review material, and if you give people prizes as they participate, everyone will get into the act.

- Divide the larger group into smaller groups and ask each group to create a list of the three most important concepts, ideas, or actions you've discussed up until that point. In order to accomplish that they'll have to review all the material you've covered. Then have each group report their lists and the material is reviewed again. (Clever, isn't it?)

Including time for reviews during a session is time well spent. Maybe you should drop Mrs. Paris a line and thank her for teaching you more than spelling.

Chris

Dear Reviewless:

There are ways of reviewing that fall into the category of nonstandard approaches, too. Read on. Some trainers with a playful bent set up "auditory anchors" for their group. That is, they repeat a phrase several times and then count on the group to take over on cue. Most of the time it works, but done too often, it can turn people off. A similar method is the sentence completion strategy, in which the trainer writes or repeats a sentence, and then asks the group, in unison, to repeat it. Again, done with restraint, this can be fun and fruitful.

There's another strategy that probably found its roots in the Dale Carnegie course; specifically, the memory improvement section. Some trainers help people remember key points by linking the ideas with visual images. Later on, only the images are shown, and participants are asked to repeat the word or idea that went with the concept. This is fun and energizing, and people seem to enjoy the surprise of learning that their memories are better than they thought. This can be done systematically, as you add one or two items to your list. Of these three strategies, this is my favorite and seems the most universally enjoyed by my groups.

Adding these tips to the suggestions Chris gave you, it will never be necessary for you to be reviewless again.

Leslie

 Dear Instant Trainers:

One of our insurance company's regular trainers invited me to a local ASTD chapter meeting. I went and watched as everyone nodded their heads when the speaker said that answering the participants' questions was really important. In the few orientation sessions I've done with our new claims adjusters, nobody has ever asked a question. Could I be doing something that stops people from asking questions?

Quiet in Quincy

Dear Quiet:

Questions are funny things. We use them to gather information, clarify instructions, and elicit opinions. The very act of asking a question, however, often makes us feel that we aren't as smart as all the people who nod their heads and don't say a word. There is an added element of fear if the person being asked the question has a higher level job than the person asking the question. Does the learner really want to say "I don't understand" to a person who could impact his or her future with the organization?

Don't be fooled. Just because people nod their heads doesn't mean they agree or understand. Head nodding can indicate understanding, but sometimes it means, "If I nod my head, maybe I won't get called on!" To confirm that learning is happening, you need to persist until you get a few questions. Here are two techniques that I've used to encourage questions.

When I ask if anyone has any questions, I remind myself to pause long enough for people to have time to think of a question and ask it. Many inexperienced trainers will say (all in one rushed breath), "Doesanyone-haveanyquestions?Okay,movingrightalong." Adults need processing time as well as time to decide to ask a question.

Another technique that works involves breaking the larger group into smaller groups and asking them to collectively come up with two or three questions about the material you've covered up until that point. Each small group presents its questions, duplicates are eliminated, and the group as a whole works on finding the answers, with you moderating the discussion and acting as their resource.

Creating an atmosphere that encourages questioning is an important skill for anyone who does training. I'm glad you asked this question.

By the way, good for you for attending an American Society for Training and Development (ASTD) meeting! There are ASTD chapters around the United States as well as international chapters. They host information-packed, helpful, and affordable meetings. To find out the chapter nearest you, call their headquarters; the contact information is in Appendix C.

Chris

Dear Quiet:

It's an awful feeling waiting for those questions to come. But you can break the quiet by assuming people will ask you questions, and waiting. Few trainers ever wait more than two or three seconds. It takes people awhile to figure out if they even have a question. Here's the easiest and quickest way to get people to ask questions: Give them the questions ahead of time. Put the questions you want to answer on index cards. Number them and put them on chairs. Ask for the number when you're ready for that question. It's called "Priming the

Pump" and it usually spawns more questions. You can imagine how difficult it is for new people to ask questions. They don't want to feel dumb or be considered dumb. Give them this "question starter kit" and they'll do the rest.

Reward those who ask questions. You don't have to give them money or big prizes, but let them know how much you appreciate their questions. That helps, too. Mostly, it's a question of helping your group give you what you want or need from them. If you set them up for success, they'll help you succeed, too. Read further on question asking and responding, and by the time you finish, things won't be so quiet anymore.

Leslie

Dear Instant Trainers:

In my head I know the importance of asking for questions. My gut is an entirely different matter. What if someone asks me a question that I can't answer? Wouldn't I lose all the credibility I've built up if I get tripped up by a trainee?

Stumped in Stanford

Dear Stumped:

Here's a good question about questions. Not having an answer isn't what robs people of credibility—bluffing an answer does!

There are two kinds of questions, those that ask for facts and those that ask for opinions. The rules for responding to each are slightly different. If you keep these distinctions in mind, I think you'll become more comfortable handling the questions posed to you during a training session.

A fact-based question should only be answered if you know the exact answer. This is no time for thinking you can bluff your way through! Your answer should be as specific as possible and should cite the source of your information. If you don't know the answer or can't remember the specifics, say something like, "That's a great question and I don't have the answer to it. At the break I'll do some checking and will get back to you with the answer then." You won't lose credibility, as long as you keep your word. You will be perceived as putting people off if you don't get back to the person after the break, at a later time, or whenever you promised. Sometimes I'll even pause for a few minutes to write the question down and put the piece of paper in my pocket so I'm sure to remember to make a call, check a record, or look something up at break time.

Opinion questions are another matter. Because you are in the front of the room, it is expected that you have thought about the subject you're discussing. Therefore, when you're asked for your opinion, give it. You don't have to answer off the top of your head. A clever response could be, "That's a great question. (Pause.) Nobody's ever asked me that before. (Pause.) Let me think for a few minutes and I'll have an answer for you." This pattern provides a gracious way to give yourself a few moments to collect your thoughts. Just as with fact-based questions, it is your responsibility to come back to the question and reply to it.

Just one more thing. Whichever kind of question you're answering, don't forget to restate the question first to be sure what you heard is what the other person said. Paraphrasing like this is a critical skill. You'll find yourself getting more comfortable doing it as you practice.

By the way, thanks for asking such a powerful question.

Chris

Dear Stumped:

Just in case you haven't thought about it, remember that you have a group of experienced adults in front of you, and if you can't answer the question, your group may be able to. There will be times when it is appropriate for you alone to give an opinion or factual answer, but there will be more times when what your group thinks or knows is equally legitimate.

If you're worried about your image, let people know ahead of time that you have an answer but you want to solicit other answers first. Then you can come back after fielding questions and state your position. This protects your image and it also lets your participants get actively involved. All too often we take our training position too seriously and we think we have to answer every question ourselves. While we're the trainers, we may have a lot of experts in our presence, and people deserve to be heard. This approach also builds your facilitation and listening skills, which can only be an asset in a work world that demands we be so many things to so many people.

Leslie

 Dear Instant Trainers:

Little did I know that our General Manager would put me in charge of guest relations in our hotel. My charge is to present a refresher course to the front desk staff. I have worked in hospitality for years, so the ideas are familiar to me, but teaching it to others is not! How do I figure out what to present, how to present it, and in what order? Please help!

Overwhelmed in Olympia

Dear Overwhelmed:

Good answers result from good questions, so let's take one step at a time. Is there a central reason your General Manager wants a refresher course or is this just a matter of course? Talk with your work associates and ask if they have any service problems or areas of need. Have you observed desk relations firsthand, or could you somehow do so without intruding, to see how guests are treated?

Here are three steps to take for locating materials you can use:

- Ask yourself what material has been most helpful for you in the past.
- Ask the General Manager if he or she has a favorite book or resource.
- Ask your associates the same questions.

There are many good books on customer service and most bookstores carry *Books in Print,* which lists books by author, title, and subject. Use this resource to compare classic works with the newest titles and determine what will be most appropriate for your purposes.

You will find a wealth of suggestions on presentation and delivery skills throughout *The Instant Trainer,* particularly Chapters 15 and 17. Relax, be yourself, enjoy the process, and learn with your learners. Incorporate a bit of humor (see Chapter 21), some handout materials, visual interest, and meaty discussion, plus some role playing (see Appendix A). Like any other task you tackle, just take a step at a time. Determining the primary need and the areas your associates are most interested in will help you select your material.

Leslie

Dear Overwhelmed:

As Leslie suggested, I would spend some time observing the front desk. Many times trainers go to the books and the students for all their information and they forget to look at things from an external perspective. Anytime you're doing training on a subject that will affect customers (either directly or indirect-ly), it's important to get their perspective. The time you spend gaining the cus-tomer perspective will be time well spent.

Chris

Dear Instant Trainers:

Imagine my surprise when our Fire Chief asked me to present a series of Fire Safety courses in our community! I've never spoken to a group before, but just think—I could be responsible for helping prevent a tragedy. Count me in! For that reason, I want to make sure people clearly understand what I'm saying. What's the best way to determine if they've actually learned what I'm teaching them? Are there any secrets you can share?

Conscientious in Columbus

Dear Conscientious:

Your question is a good one. You're teaching awareness rather than a specific skill, such as when you conduct a CPR class. To properly determine if people are "getting it," you'll need some kind of response mechanism so you can measure what people are learning. Many trainers in this position encourage participant involvement (and even excitement) by introducing the element of competition into their presentation.

Here's an example. Create a checklist of the most common fire hazards in the average home. After you have raised people's awareness levels by cit-ing statistics, showing slides of the aftermath of a fire, demonstrating with props how even heavy metals are melted in a fire, and showing various examples of fire hazards, distribute the checklist. Ask people to identify the potential hazards in their own homes, and discuss how they are going to eliminate or significantly reduce the number of hazards in their homes. You could ask for examples after the discussion, and applaud the participants' ability to both identify and correct the situation.

You could also give "prizes" to the people with the fewest items on their checklists or to those who came up with the best preventive or correc-tive measures. Prizes could consist of brochures on fire safety, first aid, CPR, poison control, and other safety tips. You are only limited by your own sense of creativity and desire to make the experience meaningful for your audience. With your level of conscientiousness, I expect you will be able to create the atmosphere you want once you grab their attention.

Leslie

Dear Conscientious:

Games are another way to check for learning. In Chapter 21 you'll find some suggestions on how to create games that fit your subject. Thanks for knowing that the trainer's job extends beyond the classroom to the real world. You've done your job when people not only enjoy your sessions, but tell you how much they can use what you taught them!

Chris

 Dear Instant Trainers:

As a postal service employee, I will soon have the opportunity to instruct employees on our new scanner technology. As I reflect back on some of my initial training experiences, my most vivid memory is that of feeling isolated and intimidated. I was afraid to ask questions or admit I was confused because I didn't want my coworkers to think I was stupid. I would like people to feel comfortable so they will talk with each other and feel free to interact and especially to ask questions. How do I go about this?

Friendly in Fresno

Dear Friendly:

How good of you to concern yourself with the comfort level of your learners. Your attitude can make or break the training session. Here are some suggestions to help put your learners at ease. Openly state that there are no dumb questions. Putting this up front in your presentation and mentioning it again midstream will help everyone feel more comfortable about asking. You might make up or disclose a "dumb question" you had about the technology prior to your training.

You could also speak to others who have conducted training on scanner technology and find out what kinds of questions arose during their sessions. You could even write down a few questions (either by making them up or gathering them from others) and go through them one by one in front of your group. This might generate additional questions.

You can also occasionally interject hypothetical statements such as, "Now you may be wondering why …" or "Perhaps it has occurred to you…." As you work with your group, watch people's faces closely. A furrowed brow, nod, tilted head, raised eyebrow, or blank look can indicate it's time for a question. Of course, the way you respond to the very first question (whatever it is!) can also influence the quantity and quality of the questions you get, so make sure you reinforce that first participator, regardless of what he or she asks. These techniques are simply common sense, but your willingness to apply them can make the difference between silent confusion and sustained interaction between yourself and your trainees.

Leslie

Dear Friendly:

One more tip. How about rewarding people for asking questions? I like to keep some Tootsie Rolls or Tootsie Pops handy (they're less than 30 percent fat) and when someone asks a question, I say, "What a great question, you deserve a reward!" You'd be amazed how many people will ask a question for a prize. While candy is dandy, there are other prizes you can use. A pencil or pen, a button, or a small company token will work just as well. The only thing to remember is that once you start giving prizes away, if you stop them, you're apt to stop the flow of questions.

Chris

Dear Instant Trainers:

Our sporting goods store has grown so much over the past five years that our staff has doubled. We are introducing a series of in-house seminars on customer service and as the Human Resources Director I get to conduct the training. This is a new role for me, but I feel fairly confident in my ability to handle it. I do have a question though, about the use of questions in my training. I don't want to get up there and act as if I'm the only one who knows this stuff.

You see, I am convinced that most of our staff understand the importance of service. I think they even know how to do it, but they don't realize how much they know. My plan is to build everyone's confidence by demonstrating that they are, in effect, service "experts." In other words, I want to facilitate rather than teach. But to be a good facilitator, I need to ask good questions so I can get good answers. My question is: What happens if I ask good questions but don't get any response? I don't want to put anyone in the hot seat (including myself). Help!

Facilitative in Flagstaff

Dear Facilitative:

Help is on the way. You're right—good questioning techniques lead to good answers, but they may not come immediately. Most people are used to being lectured at and led, and you plan to take a different approach. The first thing you need to do is get comfortable with silence. After you pose a question, wait for the answers. This may sound peculiar, but many trainers answer their own questions because they are uncomfortable with silence. Give people time to consider what you've asked.

If, after a protracted amount of time, no one has answered your question, either ask it again (using different words) or suggest a small-group discussion. Once your groups have talked for a few minutes, ask the same question again. If you still get no response, here's a tricky spin. Instead of asking, "What do you think?" or "Who has a comment?" which asks for a direct response, ask, "Who in your group had a good example?" People seem far more willing to volunteer someone else's comments (rather than their own) and it's also a nifty way to draw out those who might not otherwise participate.

You want to make it rewarding for your staff to respond to questions. You can begin by using questions that are easy to answer. Start with the most simple question of all ("Who in here is ever a customer?") and build from there. This gives people a chance to settle in, adjust to a facilitative venue, and get comfortable. Ask questions about their experiences as customers. We all have a multitude of positive and negative examples. As you progress you can make your questions more concentrated and complex.

Good facilitators maintain an attitude that says "There are no wrong answers." If you get a response that's different from what you were looking for, say, "Well, that's a possibility" or "I hadn't thought about that" or "Yes, you're right! And what else?" or "There's something additional I'm looking for." This is especially important in the beginning of a program when staff members are wondering how they'll be treated if they contribute. As you know, people's egos are fragile and you don't want to embarrass anyone or have someone feel intimidated or pressured. This is especially critical when people are with their peer group.

It's also helpful to have backup questions for times when you want to steer a person toward the answer you want. Examples include: "And what else?" or "And if that fails, what would you do?" or "And, in addition, you would want to remember to do what?" If the person seems genuinely stumped, invite others to contribute.

Here are some additional suggestions for handling silence:

- Check to make certain the group knows a question was asked.
- Rephrase the question.
- Look directly at someone you think has an answer but needs a little prodding.
- Call, by name, someone in the group whom you know to be vocal.
- Call on someone whose good comment you overheard during the discussion.

When asking a question for which you want a direct answer, make sure you:

- State the question clearly so it is easily understood.
- Be clear about your purpose: Do you want participation or to stimulate thinking?
- Act as if you expect an answer.
- Use eye contact; look intently at key individuals as you ask.
- Wait; give everyone time to process the information.

Here are some tips on addressing a specific individual in your group. (Caution: Use this judiciously. This can draw out some people and cause others to drop out!) Look at the person while you ask the question and maintain eye contact afterward. Hold for a moment, then raise your eyebrows in an inquisitive manner. Another technique is to direct the question specifically to the individual you want to respond, but make sure you say the person's name **before** you ask the question so you have his or her attention. Otherwise you may create an embarrassing situation by calling on someone who wasn't listening.

The best learning takes place when people are able to build on their knowledge and skills. Good questions are the vehicle that drives the process. I hope these ideas put you on track and keep you there!

Leslie

Dear Facilitative:

I want to go back to the idea of addressing a question to a specific individual in your session. When you use this technique, especially if it's early on in a program and the participants don't know you or your style well, monitor your tone of voice very carefully. The last thing you want to do is remind the learners of how they felt in the third grade when their least favorite teacher called on them. Keep your voice light and inviting, asking for an opinion ("What do you think about ..." or "How do you feel about ...") rather than demanding an answer. Once your class gets used to this approach, wonderful learning will take place for both you and them!

Chris

DELIVERING YOUR CONTENT

The medium is the message.

Marshall McLuhan

Most of us had at least one teacher from our childhood who stood out among the rest; a teacher who, by sheer example, imprinted on us a value or philosophy that has stayed with us through the years. While we we may not think about these special people every day, once in a while we remember who they were and what they taught us. What was it about these teachers that made them so unforgettable? Perhaps it was that they practiced what they preached.

The most powerful trainers are those who live their message. They have a passion for presenting, a desire to do it well, the commitment to keep getting better, and a need to make a difference. Even though their delivery may not be perfect, they exemplify and express their message explicitly not only by what they say, but by who they are as human beings. They are fully present, ready to work with their participants, and open to whichever direction the learning will take that day.

As you read this section, consider all of the different approaches for getting your ideas across and discover which will work best for you. Spend a few moments now and then trying to clarify what you're trying to accomplish and how you plan to do it. There may be times when you will feel as if you're completely responsible for everyone's learning, but your participants hold a stake in it, too. Share the responsibility for making learning happen with your group.

From designing your message to delivering it, please remember that regardless of what you're trying to communicate, much of your message will come not from *what* you say, but from *how* you say it. You are the real message, first and foremost, and all of the information you present is an extension of you. How you deliver it is important, because the message is a reflection of the messenger. When the message matches the medium, it all comes through, loud and clear.

Dear Instant Trainers:

I've gotten several letters from patients and their families thanking me for the care I've given them. Because they also sent copies to my supervisor, she decided I should share my ideas with the other aides in our nursing home at our next staff meeting. I don't want to sound like I'm lecturing them. What else can I do beside talking about giving good service?

Needy in Nashville

Dear Needy:

I remember a doctor telling me years ago that patients got better when they were actively involved in their care. I think the same thing applies to learners. The more involved a learner is in the learning process, the better the learning process is. So you're right on target when you become concerned that talking at people might not be the best way for them to learn.

One of the best ways to get people involved is to use exercises that are called *role plays*. A role play is an activity in which two or more people are assigned a part to play in a short exchange that reflects the subject of the session. Your topic of patient/family service is a natural for role playing.

Even though role playing is an effective teaching tool, not everyone is excited about participating. In fact, some people get downright nervous if you announce your intention of doing a few role plays during your session. Traditional role plays often consisted of the trainer picking two people, bringing them up to the front of the room, giving them a scenario to act out, and encouraging the audience to critique their performances. Under those circumstances, I wouldn't be too eager to do a role play either.

There are other, more effective ways to do role plays. Here's my favorite.

- Think up three situations that each involve two people that would help participants experience the points you want to make. Write a brief description of the overall situation and the roles of the two people involved.

- Divide the group into groups of three and give them the paragraph describing the scene they'll be acting out. Identify the tallest person as the observer. Ask the observer to look for positive interactions and suggestions for improvement. Assign the roles to the other two people and have them start the role play.

- After an appropriate amount of time (depending on the complexity of the scenario), bring the group back together and ask the small groups to discuss the following questions:

  1. What made this a helpful interaction?

  2. Where did we fail to communicate well?

  3. What can the observer tell us about our interaction?

- After the small groups have had the chance to talk things over, ask the group as a whole to share what they've learned.

- When you are ready for your next role play, have the groups reform, assign the role of the observer to the shortest person, and repeat the cycle. The third role play ... well, you've figured it out!

Role plays take good preparation and enthusiastic delivery. If you're willing to supply both, the impact of your presentation will increase dramatically. Good luck!

Chris

Dear Needy:

As you will see elsewhere in The Instant Trainer, *it's helpful to call your role plays Skill Practices. That way you can sort of sneak up on people and delay their anxiety. If you let people spread out in their little groups they'll feel more comfortable practicing their skills. And here's a nice way to end your debriefing periods, if you're up to it.*

I like to play my own form of Stump the Trainer. After we practice our role plays, I sit down in front of my group and ask if they have any situations they would like to role play with me. I become the "victim," (the person practicing the skills) which allows my participants to bring up a situation they've been struggling with. A participant can take the role of an angry customer, unhappy client, uncooperative employee, or whatever and I try to take the participant's work role. This is often a powerful exercise because people figure out they can really do this, with a little bit of work. They tease me that I can easily rattle off an answer and I remind them I, too, had to work at it. An additional benefit is that my participants witness me being willing to take a risk, just as I am asking them to do when they return to the workplace. It's only fair, don't you think? They need to see me lay it on the line, just as I am asking them to do!

Leslie

Dear Instant Trainers:

I got stuck with the job of explaining shipping policies to the new administrative assistants at our law firm. The sessions are boring even to me! When I asked one of our corporate trainers what I could do, she said, "Try a small group activity." How can I try something when I don't know what it is?

Bored in Biscayne Bay

Dear Bored:

Ouch! There's nothing worse in my mind (except maybe a person who consistently uses jargon) than a trainer who's bored with his or her own material. The sad fact is there's a possibility that we'll all experience the phenomenon at least once in our training lifetimes.

Let me clear up the language problem first. *Small group activity* is a generic term that covers any kind of an exercise that breaks a larger group of people into several smaller groups working on a task. The value of a small group activity comes from involvement. In a larger group, head nodding can be construed as participation. In a smaller group, more people feel comfortable voicing their opinions and sharing their ideas. The bonus is that when you get people involved in something, the overall group's, and the trainer's, energy goes up—hence the cure for boredom.

If I were in your shoes I might try something like this. After briefly explaining the new shipping policies, I'd break the group into several smaller groups of between three and five, assign one of these questions to each group, and ask them to discuss their answers. At the end of a reasonable conversation time, ask each group to share their ideas.

- What are the biggest changes we'll have to make?
- What are the most difficult changes we'll have to make?
- How can we best remind ourselves of the new policies during the learning process?

You get the idea. The easiest small group activity is discussion on specific topics by subsets of the whole group with an opportunity for the group as a whole to hear the ideas of all the smaller groups. There are hundreds of other possibilities. Check out Appendix D, Training Activities, for books that will explain them completely. No matter what small group activity you choose, if you plan it well, neither you or your participants will be bored!

Chris

Dear Bored:

Here's another way to look at this. Your participants are living, breathing people with ideas and experience. Why shouldn't they exchange some of their own ideas? Small group activities can range from building towers with Tinker Toys to drawing one's life story on a flip chart sheet. If you think back to your school experience you'll probably remember that the classes you liked the most involved some kind of activity you enjoyed. Well, adults may be different from kids in many ways, but deep inside there's still a young person trapped in that grown-up body. Put that imagination to work and your job will be easier!

The more relevant your activities, the more powerful and memorable they are. Let your participants work on some problems or challenges they face every day and they'll do the rest. You'll generate energy, commitment, and camaraderie. Peruse the McGraw-Hill Games Trainers Play *series and you'll have enough group activities to last you a lifetime.*

Leslie

Dear Instant Trainers:

Since the last thing I want to hear is a lecture, it's also the last thing I want to give. How can you deliver a body of content without talking on and on and on?

Lecture Phobic in Lansing

Dear Lecture Phobic:

A kitchenette is a small kitchen, a pipette is a small pipe, and a lecturette is both a small lecture and the answer to your excellent question. Adults do not learn effectively from vast amounts of information delivered in one beginning-to-end package. Think of dividing your content into a series of cleverly sequenced chunks of information separated by activities that enhance, illustrate, or allow opportunity for practice.

Let's say I wanted to train people on a new phone system and my content needed to include the following: why we've changed our phone system, the problems the new system will eliminate, an overview of the new system, and explanations of the most often used features. Here's what my training session could look like:

- Opening Lecturette: Why we've changed our phone system
- A Top Ten List, a la David Letterman, outlining the problems the new system will eliminate
- A Top Ten List, a la David Letterman, outlining the problems the new system will likely create (at least for the short term)
- Lecturette: An overview of the new system
- Distribution and opportunity for discussion of a new phone features cheat sheet
- Lecturette: Explanations of the most often used features
- Hands-on practice session to explore the phones' features

This kind of programming requires more, not less, preparation than a lecture. You have to be flexible, attentive to details, and responsible with time. Once you get the hang of it, you'll never go back to lecturing again!

Chris

Dear Lecture Phobic:

You've heard the old saying, "It isn't what you say, it's how you say it," and that certainly applies to how or for how long you present information. Participants will appreciate your presenting information in small, approachable bits. After all, adult learners bring a wealth of experience to your classroom and it's your job to capitalize on what they know.

Your learners bring the mortar; you supply the bricks. If they have some of their own bricks then you add the mortar. By mixing principles and techniques on both your parts, together you build the foundation. Everyone takes it from there. If you keep your points brief, organized, and relevant, your learners will consider you a great trainer. Bore them with too much talk and you'll strain their patience. Just remember to keep the "ette" in your lectures and you'll be fine!

Leslie

Dear Instant Trainers:

When my boss drafted me to prepare and deliver a telephone sales skills refresher to the agents in our office, I pulled out my notes from the sessions I've attended. As I paged through them I realized that I couldn't remember any of the trainers, but I could remember some of the stories they told. Those stories stayed with me and reminded me of some pretty important material. Can you help me be a storyteller?

Hopeful in Honolulu

Dear Hopeful:

You're right—storytelling is a powerful teaching tool. Think of the Greek myths, Aesop's fables, and Grimm's fairy tales. As soon as you remember the story, you'll remember the lesson it taught.

I've been lucky enough to associate with some of the greatest storytellers in the world—members of the National Speakers Association. Here are a few things I've learned from them.

- Great storytellers are made, not born. Oh sure, there are a few natural storytellers, but by and large, the memorable storytellers have found a way to learn this skill.

- Telling a story is not the same as telling a joke. Although humor plays an important part in many great stories, not all great stories are humorous.

- Good storytellers get their material from real life, usually their own real lives. Tempting as it may be to tell the story you hear from another presenter, it will never be as powerful as the one you could tell based on your own experience.

- Great storytellers practice, a lot. Although a story might sound completely spontaneous to the listener, the storyteller has spent hours practicing. When I've been in a situation that might become a good story, I make notes and tell it a few times (to anyone who might stand still long enough to listen) to see the reaction I get from others. If I get favorable reactions to the story, or to part of the story, I go to work perfecting it. A good story, like a good performance, is worth the effort.

- Stories that work in training sessions are always closely linked to the subject being presented or the point being made. As interesting as the story about the first time you drove a stick-shift car may be, it's probably not relevant to a lot of training issues. Just as great trainers tailor the content of their material to fit the needs of the people attending their sessions, great storytellers choose their stories for a particular section of content.

- Great storytellers listen to other great storytellers. Not, of course to copy the content of the story, but for delivery techniques and ideas. I have every one of Garrison Keillor's audio tapes from his show, *A Prairie Home Companion,* and from his many books, and I listen to them over and over.

You can be a good storyteller, Hopeful, just as long as you are willing to work at it.

Chris

Dear Hopeful:

Chris was right on when she talked about storytellers. We all have a story, or a series of them. Sometimes we worry about where our stories will come from because it doesn't feel as if we have any, but we do. Part of the process is in identifying how many experiences we encounter in our everyday lives that are the fodder for stories.

As a trainer, you not only tell stories, but you hear other people's stories. I tell my participants that all I need to be a good trainer is to have a good memory. I'm not the one who says the most brilliant things in my sessions; it is often my participants. I just need to remember what they said and know where or when to use it.

We grew up with stories. We still love them. That's why we read and watch TV—to get our share of stories. That's even why we complain, for someone to hear our story. For a really fun and touching element you can add to your training, here's a suggestion. One of these days, when you have an extra hour or so, go to a bookstore and browse through the children's section. I bet you'll find something suitable to match the topic you're presenting. I hope you'll be willing to share it with your learners!

Leslie

Dear Instant Trainers:

Using humorous props and funny items in programs is one thing, but is there ever a time when nonhumorous props may be used with any level of effectiveness? I will be promoting and teaching our new corporate wellness program and I think the visual effect of comparing particular food items (both healthy and unhealthy) could be effective, even though it won't be particularly funny. I can't say I've used this technique, but I think it could be done. In fact, in browsing through my cupboard and refrigerator, I already have a few ideas along this line. What do you think?

Well Stocked in Winston-Salem

Dear Well Stocked:

Indeed, props go far beyond encounters of the humorous kind. I have seen nutritionists compare various food items, and I agree that visuals can add a special real-life element to your wellness program. I once watched a presenter create a huge pile of raw potatoes that equaled the caloric value of one small order of french fries. It was a powerful visual.

Public health nutritionists who work with low-income families often use plastic models of food to demonstrate what a four-ounce portion of meat looks like, or what constitutes a serving of vegetables. If you have any kind of imagination (and it appears that you do), you could create a series of powerful props that your audience members will not only remember but appreciate. I hope this encouragement whets your appetite for unlimited portions of creativity!

Leslie

Dear Well Stocked:

Whoever said "A picture is worth a thousand words" was right. Anytime a trainer can back up words with a visual and make it something a participant can touch or manipulate, the learning will be increased!

Chris

 Dear Instant Trainers:

Since our Personnel Department was recently downsized, I became an instant benefits expert. Only I'm not an expert! My knees are still knocking from my first employee orientation last week. People asked a lot of questions I couldn't answer because the answers can change on a day-to-day basis. When I was in high school, I was taught that a quick way to lose your credibility is to say, "I don't know." So what should I do when people ask questions I can't answer?

Can't in Kankakee

Dear Can't:

You're right; being a benefits expert is almost a contradiction in terms. But being an expert doesn't mean you have to know it all. You are the victim of an old myth and it's time to liberate yourself from the past. You can actually gain credibility by saying, "I don't know" if you follow it with the phrase, "but I'll find out for you!" It's far better to admit you don't know than to fake it. The ability to honestly admit we don't know (and do it with comfort) is rare. But the finding out part? That's where you can make your credibility soar. Make a promise, and deliver. Even in instances when you are unable to find the answer, letting people know that up front is an asset, too.

The critical factor is follow-up. Make a note of the question and the person asking it and promise to follow up. Your prompt response time (whether you have the answer or not) will make you look like an expert every time! Who could ask for more benefits than that?

Leslie

Dear Can't:

There's a big difference between questions that ask for facts and those that ask for an opinion. Leslie's right, never bluff on a fact question—it will come back to haunt you. Opinion questions are another matter. Here's where the title of expert comes in. If you are in front of a group, they have the right to believe that you've spent time caring and thinking about the subject you're discussing. Therefore, you need to be able to express an opinion on these kinds of questions. In your position as a company spokesperson you do need to be very specific so learners know the difference between your opinions and your company's policies.

Chris

Dear Instant Trainers:

As a manufacturing manager, I realize that workplace safety is a big issue in our plant. When I conduct a training session on safe and proper work practices, I want to make sure the message sticks. What techniques or strategies could I implement that will help employees actually practice what they are learning?

Safe in Sarasota

Dear Safe:

The past helps influence the future. Can you offer a brief historical perspective on work safety in your plant, or in manufacturing in general? Perhaps you have some riveting statistics that will impress the importance of safety on your employees. Do you post signs of your safety record? The most effective are the positive ones, such as prominent signs announcing the number of days or months without a lost-time accident (rather than "We have had *X* accidents so far this year."). The positive statistic gives everyone a new goal to work toward. This can bring out a competitive desire to beat the old number and to continue increasing the time between accidents.

In your safety presentation, after presenting your material, you could distribute some brief case studies with a "what's wrong with this" approach. Let small groups read and discuss the situation. If you have slides, an overhead, or an LCD panel, you could show photographs of unsafe practices and have participants identify what's wrong (similar to what we did in coloring books as kids). You could give prizes to the teams that identify the most incorrect practices.

You could organize "investigative teams" to identify unsafe practices on the floor and report on how they corrected them. You could have departments cooperate in a safety campaign complete with team names, logos, slogans, etc. Most people get into the spirit of things when they are asked to organize, compete, or create a campaign. These approaches have proven to be a safe bet for others; we hope they will work for you.

Leslie

Dear Safe:

It is a good (I almost said safe) bet that without some form of practice, messages won't stick for very long. Some kinds of training provide easy opportunities for practice. Safety training doesn't. How about providing coffee and donuts for a few of your employees and asking them for their ideas on how a training session could afford opportunities for meaningful practice? They might give you a few great ideas.

Chris

GETTING PEOPLE TO PARTICIPATE

What is the sound of one hand clapping?

Buddhist Proverb

How many of us, when we receive that envelope in the mail that reads, "You may already be a winner!" simply throw it away without checking the contents? More likely, we tear it open, speed-read the big print, and carefully follow the instructions, hoping for fame and fortune (or at least fortune!) as we return the envelope with what we hope is our lucky number. Someone asked us to participate, and we did.

Now, you're not Ed McMahon or Dick Clark, and you can't offer the people who attend your programs a million dollars in prizes, but you can promise them a truly valuable experience if they are willing to participate in the process. It's not always easy getting people to do what you ask of them; not everyone is comfortable working in groups. But if you simply invite people to take an active role in learning, and help them to feel this will be a positive and fruitful experience, they may just cooperate.

Participation occurs at many levels: Some people may be loners while others are more gregarious. Some are silent, active thinkers where others need to talk things over before they can learn. Some work well in groups and others are disappointed at being asked to do so. Everyone is just a little bit different.

Your job as a trainer is to help combine the best of everyone's differences and bring out their best through active engagement in learning. This section features strategies for getting participation, which can range from simply raising one's hand in response to a question to helping facilitate an in-depth discussion. They are also means by which you can gauge the effectiveness of your message and methods. People are willing to participate in an activity when they think there's something in it for them, something to be gained or gotten. Imagine how exciting life would be for both the trainer and trainees if we believed ongoing learning was as valuable as a sweepstakes prize!

With this in mind, when your participants begin walking through the door, you can look at them and smile, because you know something they might not know yet: Each and every one of them is a winner!

 Dear Instant Trainers:

I am the new volunteer coordinator for an office that offers special services for older and retired citizens. After a few years of semiretirement, I started missing being around people, but that's all behind me now. It's my job to welcome, orient, and train new volunteers, and I need to get my training skills polished up in record time. This may sound funny, but I actually feel pretty comfortable with the part about delivering content; as a former teacher, I think this will come naturally. What I'm hesitant about is how to help everyone feel comfortable and a part of things. You know how it is. Some people are more outgoing than others, and some are downright shy. How can I get people to talk to each other so everyone will feel comfortable in my sessions?

Warm Welcome in Westchester

Dear Warm Welcome:

I'm going to give you the short answer first and then I'll give you a longer one, too. The short answer is, if you want people to talk to each other, tell them to talk to each other. It's really that simple. You'll be amazed that in a training session, most people will do just about anything you ask within reason. As you get more comfortable, you'll find that even when you ask participants to do something just a bit outrageous, they'll do it!

The only caution is that you must be clear on what you want them to do. The better your instructions, the better the results (look for the comments on giving instructions in Chapter 13).

Now for the longer part of the answer. If you want to help people relax and get acquainted, find a series of icebreakers, participative introductions, and group activities you think will fit your group. There are some great books on icebreakers listed in Appendix D, and you can also read the section on Back Pocket exercises in Appendix B for quick tips on getting people to mingle. Icebreakers are easy to find and easy to create once you understand the formula.

Icebreakers are most effective when they have a purpose. For your purpose, you could ask people to share their names, what their backgrounds are, why they decided to volunteer their time and talents, how they chose your particular agency, and what they'd like to get out of the experience. Now you see how easy it is to create an icebreaker. I hope you get the sense that it really doesn't take much to get most people to participate. Just remember to give clear instructions and make the icebreaker match your purpose. If you keep these two points in mind, your group will do just about anything you ask. I'm so glad you asked this question!

Leslie

Dear Warm Welcome:

Finding and leading the right icebreaker with a group is one of the best moments in training. Right before your eyes, a group of strangers connect and start having fun. Hey, it doesn't get much better than that. You'll enjoy taking the time to research icebreakers that are beyond the "What's your name and why are you here?" model. I like to use icebreakers that force people to get up and move around. This seems to break down barriers quickly and tells me a lot about how eager people are apt to be when asked to do other activities. Your time spent getting a group off to a well-connected start will be well worth it!

Chris

Dear Instant Trainers:

I just finished my first customer service training for all of the Guest Services employees in our hotel, and it went pretty well except that people
seemed to get restless at one point. It wasn't time for a break and we had
more material to cover, so I didn't stop. I wasn't sure what to do! I felt a bit
awkward about the incident, like there was something I could or should
have done, but my boss was sitting in the room and giving everyone a
break was out of the question. Based on your extensive experience, how do
you handle these kinds of situations?

Tired in Tupelo

Dear Tired:

Every trainer who conducts programs over one hour in length has
experienced this dilemma, and yes, there are some options other than
breaks. The easiest one is to stop after having made an important point (or
a series of them) and let participants "absorb" the material by discussing it
for a few moments. It couldn't be simpler.

Explain that you want them to remember this information, and ask
them to talk with a partner or in a small group (three or four) about what
they consider to be the most important point(s) made so far and how they
can personally apply the information. Keep in mind that two people talking
together takes less time than four. Asking everyone to stand up for their discussion offers both a mental and physical break, and "ups" the energy level
immediately.

Here's another idea if you have already done the "discussion thing."
Simply ask people to stand up and stretch out. Do not use the word "break"
or some folks will leave the room! Preface the activity by stating that you
want to do a quick "pick-me-up" to help them stay alert. Once people are on
their feet, I ask them to take a nice, deep breath from their diaphragms. I
then ask them to raise their right arms and slowly stretch them upward, then
to do the same with their left arms. I remind them to take a nice, deep
inhaling breath on the stretch and to exhale on the way down. I ask them to
stretch both arms, then engage in a single "clap."

We repeat the clap, then I ask them to do the same behind their backs
(This is fun—most people don't do this very well!). We repeat the back clap
three times and they get better by the last one (the clap gets louder)

because they've stretched themselves out. Last, I ask them to just "shake" their bodies for a moment to get the kinks out. They sit back down and get back to work. This takes no more than two minutes and I can feel the restored energy in the room.

I also use this exercise as a metaphor, explaining to participants that learning requires stretching our skills and abilities, and pointing out that our first attempts to change or improve may be marginal, but if we keep working on it, we get better. So not only does this activity offer a quick refresher for anyone whose energy has flagged, but you can also tie it into the learning process.

Leslie

Dear Tired:

I'll add one more wake-em-up activity to your repertoire: the Group Shoulder Rub. Just as Leslie suggested, don't call it a break; just ask people to stand up and push in their chairs. You are ultimately going to want people to get into one (or two) straight lines with everyone looking in the same direction. Instruct them to face the left wall and walk forward until they are an arm's length away from the person in front of them. Ask them to put their hands on the shoulders of the person in front of them and give that person a brief shoulder rub. After a few minutes ask the group to turn and face the right wall and repeat the process (this takes care of the people at each end of the row). You'll be amazed as you feel the group's energy level return. Invite people to take a deep breath, shake out the kinks, and get ready to get back to work.

Chris

Dear Instant Trainers:

I work for a lesser-known airline and have been designated as a new customer service trainer because I receive so many complimentary letters and cards from our customers. Not only will I be speaking to our employees, but for public relations purposes, our general manager is thinking about having me speak to selected companies outside of our industry, too. I think I can handle this; after all, every time I deliver a passenger briefing on a full flight I'm speaking to a hundred people or so.

Here's where I need your help: I plan to occasionally get people into small groups so they can discuss some of my ideas and practice them. I have some concerns about this because when I have been the participant and various trainers have gotten us into groups, there are sometimes "left-over people."

What can I do when I have stragglers here and there with no one to talk with? How do I handle it if someone is seated far away from a group and no one bothers to draw them in? I've been there, Instant Trainers, and I hate sitting all alone while everyone else is having fun. Even more than that, I hate having to barge in on people who have already begun their discussion. How do you handle stragglers and odd numbers so that no one feels left out?

Oddball in Ocala

Dear Oddball:

How perceptive! You've brought up an excellent point. In groups of one hundred or more this is a really hard factor to control, but you can include a special request with your instructions. When you ask people to get into groups, suggest that they look around and see if there's anyone nearby who needs to be included. Tell them to invite the individual to join their group. This will reduce the likelihood of some poor soul's being isolated from the action.

You can use this same approach in smaller groups, and with fewer people you can intervene and encourage the lone person to join a group. I've even sat down with the one "odd" person in a group and initiated the same discussion everyone else is having.

Some people wonder why all this fuss over the "odd person out," so here's why. Nobody likes rejection, and more often than not, being left out of a group can conjure up all kinds of bad memories from childhood about when we were excluded, rejected, or ridiculed. With so many of us having experienced these kinds of traumas, it would seem appropriate to prevent a flashback if we can. Most of us are not alone in our wanting to belong.

Leslie

Dear Oddball:

One more suggestion. Pay attention to where you're standing as people are pairing up. Make sure your position gives you as wide a view of the room as possible. As people are getting into their groups, your job is to wander around or watch for those who look like they're having difficulty connecting. When you find a lost soul, you can lead them to a group and do the connecting. Your participants will appreciate your efforts to make them feel a part of things.

Chris

Dear Instant Trainers:

As a seasoned participant of many, many training programs, I have really grown tired of trainers' inability to "really connect" with their audiences. I've seen attitudes range from indifferent to insulting. The cursory "Good comment" or absent-minded "Thank you" to a participant's contribution gets me. It's obvious these are just words and have no meaning behind them.

I am especially turned off by trainers who discourage participation. They treat questions as interruptions rather than as part of the learning process. In a parental tone they say, "Hold your comments until later" or "I don't want to answer any questions right now" as if the learners shouldn't get actively involved. It sends me up the wall. If I have to be a trainer I want to be a good one. How can I come across as open, interested, and sincere? I want to respect my audience so they will respect me. Any tips?

Sincere in Springfield

Dear Sincere:

I would like to commend you on the respect you feel for your participants. Yes, there are trainers who can deliver the goods but are bad at connecting with their audiences. Maybe they're trying to stick to a script and they have difficulty getting back on track after being interrupted. Yet, like many other jobs today, the trainer's job **is** to be interrupted!

Here are some tips on staying connected with your learners. First, expect to be interrupted. Pay attention to your facial expression and body language. When a person asks a question or makes a comment, look alert and interested. If someone asks a difficult or naive question, keep your facial expression neutral. Face the person squarely. Some trainers don't turn their bodies to face whomever is speaking, and this makes them look as if they are ready to flee.

Should someone ask a question at an inconvenient time, ask the person to write it down so it can be addressed later. When you finish your lecture bit, immediately go back to the question. Learners will know you're sincere, if, after you answer a question, you ask if the person feels satisfied with your response. If someone asks you something you don't know, admit it. Ask your participants if they have an answer. If it's your role to look it up, state that you will do so.

If, in your earnest desire to answer all questions and comments, you lose track and can't remember where you were, ask your group. Someone will remember. The advantage of staying connected with your audience is that you'll get plenty of support in return. It's simply a matter of remembering that you are all in this together, and that most training sessions are a process of give and take.

When receiving comments and contributions, vary your responses. Instead of always saying the same thing, have several ways of reacting. This way you come across as alert, sincere, and interested in what everyone has to say. One last thought: If you find yourself running out of time because you've spent so much time answering questions, let your group know that you have some important points to make before you wrap up. Offer to hold Q & A at the end of your session (or even afterward, one on one) so people know their concerns will be addressed. These strategies aptly reflect the old saying, "People don't care how much you know until they know how much you care."

Leslie

Dear Sincere:

*Have you ever heard of the parking lot technique? It's a great way to handle questions that are asked at an inconvenient time or are a bit off the track of the current subject. Even better, it's simple to use. Take a flip chart sheet, tape it to a wall near the front of the room, and label it **The Parking Lot**. (I often cut out a picture of a car from a magazine and paste it on for a little color.) When someone asks a question that needs to be deferred, give that person a Post-it note and ask him or her to jot down the question and "park it" in the parking lot.*

Explain that the question is too important to be forgotten, but that general subject will be covered later in the session and you want to make sure that the question isn't lost! Then, at the appropriate time, walk over to the parking lot, pull off the question, and answer it. People will really appreciate your attention to their needs and will be happy to wait till a later time, if you prove you won't forget them!

Chris

 Dear Instant Trainers:

You probably know, even better than I, that not all trainees are excited about learning. I would describe the prevailing attitude of many of my trainees as terminally reluctant. Most of the time they come around, but by then the session is almost finished. I would like create an environment that encourages people to listen, learn, and participate early on. What words of wisdom do you have for me?

Ready in Roswell

Dear Ready:

While it would be nice to think that everyone is ready to roll up sleeves and participate, that just isn't true. Sometimes it's the corporate culture, the time of day, the topic, the presenter, the personality of the group, or all of the above. But don't get discouraged.

If you want to create a participative environment, read this entire chapter carefully.

One way to begin is by making your room look and feel different. For example, avoid the standard classroom setting. Try round tables instead. Or use only chairs, or no chairs! Sit on the floor. Put posters on the walls. Have inexpensive toys on the table (Slinkies, kaleidoscopes, small tops, modeling clay, bubble liquid, yo-yos, crayons, paddle balls, or whatever are your favorites). Give token prizes to those who do participate.

Begin your presentation with some kind of audience interaction, one that fits with your topic or purpose. Include in your handout materials a series of questions that need to be asked and addressed. If people seem reluctant to get involved, precede Q & A with a brief discussion in pairs or small groups. Use participatory exercises throughout your presentation (the McGraw-Hill *Games Trainers Play* series is chock-full of examples).

If people seem reluctant to express themselves, ask them to write down their own questions or ideas on index cards and review them with the whole group (see Appendix B for more index card strategies).

People tend to participate when they think there's some kind of payoff. Your enthusiasm for your topic can spark some energy. Read Chapter 21, Putting Fun in Your Training, to get things going. Don't give up! If you try something that works well, remember it for the next time. The main thing is to stay focused on what you are there to do and to do your best. When you give the best you have to offer, your group will usually give it back in some way or another.

Leslie

Dear Ready:

One of the hardest things for new trainers is learning how to "read" participants. I remember early in my career having a woman sitting in the front row of a session with a face that had only one expression, which I thought meant "I don't want to be here!" I worried about her for the entire session. After it was over, she came up to me and said, "Thanks a million. That was the best training session I've ever attended." I thought to myself, I wish you had told your face!

Read the questions and answers in Chapter 18 about evaluating your sessions and put some of those techniques to use. By using evaluations you'll get a better sense of what the group wants or needs, and their estimation of your program.

Chris

 Dear Instant Trainers:

In three days I will be conducting my first negotiation skills training session for other reps in our union. I expect some of my participants will have some personal issues and concerns they will voice and I want to encourage them to speak up. Something tells me that there is more to training than simply getting up and speaking. I don't have time to take a course on listening skills, but if you have a few quick tips, I'd love to hear them.

Attentive in Austin

Dear Attentive:

You've already cleared the first hurdle, and that is recognizing the importance of listening in the classroom. Half of good listening is in asking good questions. Write down a few good questions ahead of time in your workbook or notes. That way, you don't have to worry about your mind going blank at the wrong time (as if there's a right time!). When participants speak, make a concentrated effort to listen for both words and feelings. Observe the speaker carefully. Note how she or he behaves while describing a situation or asking a question.

Few people realize that good listening requires a watchful eye. Nuances (body language, facial expression, hesitation, posture, breathing patterns) often tell you more than words. When a person asks a question, make sure you understand what is being asked before you answer. Verify what was said by rephrasing the question in your own words. You can then ask, "Is this what you are asking?" Pay attention to your voice tone, however, so you don't sound judgmental or as if you are challenging what the person said.

If you sense that someone is annoyed by your attempt to listen or clarify, explain your desire to answer the question you were asked and state that you like to validate before you respond. If you're confused by something someone says, ask for clarification. Say something like "I'm a little confused …" or "Just a minute; I'm a little lost …" rather than "You're confusing me …" or "You lost me there…." This way, you maintain responsibility for your interpretation rather than making the other party responsible for your lack of understanding.

If you really want to impress your learners, remember what people said or asked earlier in the program and refer to it from time to time (of course, you only want to use positive examples). People love it when you remember their situation! These listening skills will not only help you display interest in your participants, but will also help you demonstrate what true listening is all about.

Leslie

Dear Attentive:

My mentor, Marilyn Berger, taught me to remember the importance of listening with a simple statement. She said there's a reason we were given two ears and one mouth—so we can listen twice as much as we speak. The hardest thing for me when it comes to listening (and I suspect I share this with other highly verbal people), is to keep listening. I usually get the gist of the question and mentally begin preparing my reply. This is a pattern that makes it highly unlikely you'll pick up the nuances of the question. So stay focused on the questioner until he or she is done—you'll make Marilyn proud!

Chris

 ### Dear Instant Trainers:

I'm realistic enough to recognize that many of my participants are less than enthralled to be in my orientation sessions. They tend to think of them as just another meeting. You see, we are a government regulatory agency, so it's not as if I can grab their attention with sales figures or impressive marketing strategies, but I do want them to positively identify with our work. Any suggestions on how I can gain their attention and participation early on and keep it? I am determined to leave a positive impression so people will understand the importance of what we do and how citizens benefit from our efforts.

Resolved in Roanoke

Dear Resolved:

I am impressed you want to impress your employees with the importance of their work. Your agency exists for a reason, and whether your specialty is public health, workplace safety, environmental regulations, licensing, or whatever, you are right to take pride in what you do. Statistics about your agency can be an attention getter. Think of the statistics that might exist if your agency didn't! What if you wrote up some statistics on 3×5 cards (one per card) and set them on chairs before your participants file into the room. Later on you could ask individuals to read what is on their cards and you could fill in the details.

If your function is regulation, cover examples of recent citations or violations and potential outcomes. Photographs, images, or even a brief video will reinforce your message. So will props, which for a regulatory agency could range from a piece of physical evidence to a document citing multiple violations.

A "take home" fact sheet on your agency could help instill a sense of pride in what you do and how you do it. Keep in mind that your personal commitment, enthusiasm, and dedication will come through loud and clear. If you feel strongly about your agency's function, it will come across to your group, and they might just walk out of your orientation session with a renewed sense of purpose.

Leslie

Dear Resolved:

Leslie's right—helping people see the value of their work in a tangible way is crucial. How about a Little Known Facts sheet or a Did You Know card to start off your session? Maybe you could tape record some comments from citizens (dare I say customers?) who have some positive things to say about your agency, or a few words about how their lives were impacted when they didn't get the assistance they needed. Playing a few minutes of live recordings could have a great impact. The time you spend planning this opening will pay dividends in participation.

Chris

Dear Instant Trainer:

You've outlined some good strategies for encouraging group participation in this book. I'm friendly, sincere, and willing to work at creating good group interaction. But if you have any additional ideas on what it takes to invite learners to be actively involved in the process, I'd like to know them. What else do you have up your sleeves?

Sleeveless in Seattle

Dear Sleeveless:

So nice of you to ask! Generally, people are willing to participate if they trust you and if they trust that their comments will be accepted, or at least considered. Here are a few additional thoughts on encouraging participation.

Reward the first person who speaks even if he or she doesn't say anything particularly brilliant. I've seen whole groups shut down when the first person who opened his or her mouth was treated rudely by an inept trainer. Keep in mind that everyone is watching and deciding whether they want to be in on the action.

If you don't mind being obvious, set things up ahead of time by using a couple of ringers. Here's what I mean. Get acquainted with some of your early arriving participants and ask one or two outgoing individuals if they would be willing to participate. Hand them your questions or comments written out on index cards and ask them to read what's on their cards at specified times during your session.

Here's one of my personal favorites. Walk around and casually listen in on conversations while group members are discussing an assigned topic. If you happen to hear a good comment or question, let the person know you would like everyone to hear what was said when you get back into the whole group. Elsewhere in *The Instant Trainer* we mention the effectiveness of asking what good ideas came out of a group discussion because people are always happy to volunteer someone else's comments rather than their own.

If you have a touchy subject to cover and want participation, here's an idea. Pass out some index cards, ask people to write their questions or concerns on the card, and let everyone know they do not have to sign the cards. Ask your participants to pass the cards back to you. You can scan them, organize them and use the information on the cards as prompters to encourage a Q &A period, group discussion, or team project. Try to respond in general terms, however, so no one situation or person is singled out.

Purposeful participation makes a training session fun and effective. Always keep your purpose in mind and continue looking for new approaches. Most participation strategies require little on your part except for creativity. I bet you'll come up with some great ones on your own.

Leslie

Dear Sleeveless:

I often use the expression "with risk comes reward" early in a session. I explain that learning is a risky business. You might have to confess to not knowing something, you might have to try something and fail at it—both risky behaviors. Then I mention that I think risk takers in the classroom are smart people. It's better to try something in the classroom and fail than to try it on a customer, coworker, or spouse! So, I explain that people can expect to be rewarded for smart risking taking—asking a question, volunteering for an exercise, or offering a differing opinion—and I reward them with small tokens or miniature candy bars. The reward itself isn't important. As my friend and master trainer Merry Soyck said, "Even adult professionals will kill for a bag of M&M's." It's the thought that counts.

Chris

 Dear Instant Trainers:

I am part owner in a new health club in a large metropolitan area. We think of ourselves as "small but mighty" and plan to offer the best in equipment, service, and education so that local residents will choose our facility over the others in town. We are competing with some of the national chains so it's important that we do it right the first time out, or we may not have a second chance. We plan to offer a special service: Our trainers will work with our members as if they were the members' personal trainers. I volunteered to train our employees on how to help people train (work out). I've read a couple of McGraw-Hill books on training and think I have a pretty good handle on the delivery part. Of course, I know my field, having worked in the fitness industry for many years. Here's my problem. Some of our employees think they know how to teach people and I know they have more to learn. I want us all to learn in this process and figure I need to make learning both fun and rewarding. What do you suggest along the lines of rewarding my trainees so they in turn can do the same when they're instructing our members?

Pumped in Palm Springs

Dear Pumped:

It's astute of you to recognize the importance of making learning a rewarding experience. Surely it's something your members need or they wouldn't be willing to work out so hard. So you can rest easy in knowing you already have the first component of rewarding learning and that is your positive attitude. You sense the importance of celebrating an individual's insights and inroads. Acknowledgement follows. Recognize good behavior with a compliment or positive reinforcement of some sort (as I did in the beginning of my response!). You can say something like, "That's a great point; thank you!" or "I'm impressed that you were able to …" Of course, your comments need to be sincere, and the more operational they are, the better the chance they'll be repeated. Describe the behavior so the person knows exactly what he or she said or did that was so important or effective.

You can establish rewarding little rituals for when learning takes place. I've seen groups that all clap once when someone says something brilliant, or all respond with an enthusiastic "Yes!" You can buy inexpensive token gifts to give away (headbands, wristbands, energy bars, shoelaces, stopwatches, booklets on fitness and wellness, electrolyte replacement drinks) or certificates for low-end items at a favorite health food store (or your own if you sell products). You can assemble people into teams and assign points for certain learning levels (like fitness levels). Considering the business you're in, the competition element might work extremely well with your group.

There's no limit to what you can do, depending on your budget and ingenuity, but in my opinion, the one most rewarding element of all is the satisfaction you feel and exhibit when someone "gets it." Learning is fun and deserves to be rewarded, and I hope some of these suggestions will fit into your program.

Leslie

Dear Pumped:

We promised that the ideas in The Instant Trainer *would be no- or low-cost winners. Allow me to slip in one that might fit your situation perfectly, but could involve more significant dollars than a few Tootsie Rolls: You could pay people more when they learn more. There is a hotel chain that increases salaries from 10 to 25 cents per hour for employees who successfully complete specific training programs. Talk about motivating the learner! Organizations that use this kind of system believe that when employees learn a new skill and demonstrate that they're using it, they become more valuable to the company and the company should reward that. This may be beyond what you're thinking about now, but keep it in mind for the future.*

Chris

POLISHING YOUR DELIVERY SKILLS

Half of success is just showing up.

Woody Allen

Artists, musicians, athletes, writers, and award-winning actors all have one thing in common: They put in hours and hours of practice every day. They show up, rehearse, drill, practice, perform, and push themselves to do even better, time and time again. For anyone who wants to improve in a job, it's the same process. It takes dedication, time, and energy to do anything well. You've watched ice skaters dancing across the rink, making it all look so easy. But what looks so smooth and flawless today took years of practice, with many obstacles to overcome along the way.

Polishing your delivery skills takes time and effort. You may have a strong sense of what you want to say and how you'll say it; you may have a vision of what you want to do when you get in front of your next group so you can be just a little bit better next time. Slow, steady improvement is the secret to your success.

Just as your participants learn from you, so can you learn from others. Over the next few months, observe every trainer or speaker you can and determine what they do that makes them effective (or ineffective). As you conduct your trainings, show up mentally and physically. Pay attention to how your learners respond to your material, or exactly how you deliver it from one time to another, and the different impact it has on participants. Read your evaluations and heed the helpful comments.

You've probably noticed that some trainers seem to have a sixth sense for what their group needs. This appears intuitive, but it's actually an internalized ability to draw from one's own experience and apply it appropriately. This section will help you drastically shorten your learning curve and make you look more experienced than you are. It would be to your advantage if you reviewed this section every now and then. With practice, the skills you now have to consciously think about will come naturally, and people will tell you how easy you make it all look, just like the rest of the pros.

 Dear Instant Trainers:

Another nursing coordinator and I are about to do a first session on triage for our emergency department admitting staff. I've done two or three brief in-services in the past, but I've never done it with another person. The two of us are good friends so there's no threat of competition between us. In fact, we'd each bend over backwards to help out the other. We'd just like to know what's different about team teaching and what special considerations exist when one is sharing the floor with another. Can you help us?

Doubled Over in Dover

Dear Doubled Over:

Indeed, you can double your fun when you have a partner, because not all of the pressure is on you. Of course, there are some aspects unique to team teaching and I'll be happy to cover them. As you can expect, team teaching requires preparation so the two of you can work together smoothly, orchestrating your content and process, playing off each other's expertise, and offering a unified approach to your topic. It's great that there is no hint of competition between the two of you, as this tends to distract trainees.

The major considerations in team teaching are:

coequality,

preparation, and

coordination.

In opening your in-service, you can easily maintain equality by either: a) introducing yourselves individually, or b) introducing each other. If one of you handles both introductions ("This is who I am and here is my partner"), the introducer will be perceived as the "leader" or senior trainer. By keeping your roles equal in the beginning, you will set the precedent of coequality and you will be perceived as a team. The two of you can take turns explaining administrivial matters (enrollment forms, introductions, program agenda, time frames, etc.). Just make sure both of you have exactly the same information. It undermines your credibility if one of you gives improper or contradictory information that the other must correct. This gives the impression that you are unprepared.

If the intention is for you and your team teaching partner to have equal status, then share the stage equally. Participants will look for indicators of status between the two of you. Both of you will want to share responsibilities such as passing out materials, shutting off lights, arranging the room, etc., so it doesn't look as if one person is giving orders and the other is carrying them out.

Here are my thoughts on preparation. Some training partners work together so closely that they complement each other's remarks on an ongoing basis. One person talks, the other agrees, expands, and embellishes. This can be especially fun for the trainers because it is dynamic and synergistic, but it can be distracting for the audience unless they've been oriented to the process. Some people feel annoyed when one instructor "interrupts" the other. So how do you handle this? If this tends to be your approach, explain it ahead of time. People will be more relaxed about it. Participant anxiety levels go up when they think competition exists between the instructors.

The two of you can decide ahead of time who will be the primary presenter for different segments of your program. Choose by whatever criteria the two of you establish, and stick to it. This allows the secondary presenter freedom to add comments, embellish, or ask questions for the benefit of your participants. The two of you simply need to organize your material (who covers what and when) and time requirements (how long each of you will have for each segment). Do not usurp each other's time. Coordinate these items ahead of time and both of you will have less to worry about during the training itself.

While we're on the topic of coordination, it's a good idea to decide upon a system of private signals for when it's time to move on, switch gears, or take a break, or time for the secondary partner to clam up (this prevents either of you taking over the class or dominating your partner's time). Do explain to the group that the secondary instructor will intervene from time to time, and that is a part of the process. If you forget to explain this, participants may perceive that you are interrupting each other.

These are the most important three concepts behind team teaching. Of course, there may be some instances when you'll team teach with someone whose presentation style and preferences differ from yours, but if the two of you are cooperative, you'll be able to work it out. Just remember to let your group know ahead of time how you plan to work together, and the two of you will learn as you go. For now, with the opportunity to work with someone who is so compatible, the two of you will probably enjoy it so much that as soon as your in-service ends, you'll want to do it all over again!

Leslie

Dear Doubled Over:

Please notice that you addressed your letter to the Instant Trainers, not the Instant Trainer. Leslie and I have presented together and with other trainers over the years and have learned a few lessons. Training with a partner, co-facilitating, or team teaching (whatever you choose to call it) is either your worst nightmare or your best dream. I've experienced both.

It's a nightmare when you don't plan enough, don't trust enough, or don't care enough. It's a dream when you share values, respect each other, and have an equal passion for your subject. That, however, is philosophy and as you've noticed there isn't much of that in this book. In this case, don't breeze by the philosophy. All the preparation will fall by the wayside if you and your partner have differences that cause friction. Trust me, people in your session will pick up on it and the quality of the learning will suffer! But there is practical stuff to do. You need to plan, practice, and participate together.

Leslie's covered the planning and the practicing, so I'll add a few words (like a good partner would) about participating together. I believe that team training is different than two trainers each doing sections of the training materials. I always feel uncomfortable watching the trainer who isn't leading a sec-

tion of the session leaving the room to make phone calls, sitting in the back of the room working on something else, or looking generally bored. In a true partnering effort, at any given time, one trainer has the lead role and one does the supporting activities. These supporting activities include monitoring the logistics, watching the student's reactions, and offering brief comments when appropriate.

You and your friend will need to put in a few extra hours getting ready for this session. It will be worth it. I believe you can have your friendship and train together too!

Chris

Dear Instant Trainers:

The owner of the bookstore where I work has decided to introduce a series of public programs: Each employee is expected to present a brief lecture on an author of our choice. I've never done anything like this before, but I'm game. Not only am I willing, I'm excited to take on a new challenge. But if I'm going to do something like this, I want to do a good job. For my benefit, what would you describe as your three biggest "do's" and "don'ts" of presenting before a group?

Curious in Concord

Dear Curious:

What a great opportunity for everyone in your bookstore to enhance their presentation skills, and how nice that you get to choose your subject. Right away this points you toward success! Here are three "do's" that will enhance your skills immediately:

1. Do review every presenter you've ever observed and analyze what they did right (so you can do it, too) and what they did wrong (so you can avoid it). This in itself is an instant course on speaking before groups.

2. Do go into the experience with a positive attitude. Enjoy the entire process, from preparation to presentation to the wrap-up. Bring your entire personality and style into the process by choosing an author and a work you are excited about. Inspire your audience with your passion for the topic.

3. Do handle the glitches with grace. You may start late. Prepare for this ahead of time by having a small piece of your presentation you can drop if you must. Avoid complaining about anything that goes wrong. Did only three people show up? Get excited about it; this means you can have more of a conversation than a formal presentation. In other words, whatever happens, go with it. Be flexible. And if you make a mistake, learn from it and let it go. Your audience will forgive you. So forgive yourself.

These three "do's" are sufficient; the "don'ts" would be the opposite: don't forget to prepare by building on your legitimate experience, don't be negative, and don't get upset over anything that goes wrong. If you're really curious about the application of these principles, you'll probably find that they apply to more situations than giving presentations—an added benefit of your asking a good question!

Leslie

Dear Curious:

I'll add one more do to Leslie's list: Do figure out the best way for you to have some notes to work from. Since I used the word notes rather than manuscript, you've discovered my bias. Speakers who read their presentations probably don't make your top ten list of speakers to emulate! Think of your presentation as a conversation with people. What will they be most interested in learning about your subject? How can you tell them the things that will make them curious to learn more or read more? Put your answers into an outline or on some index cards. Practice using your notes as a guide, and have fun.

Chris

Dear Instant Trainers:

Next week I will do the first training session of my life. So far, I have found the organization and preparation stages challenging, but not insurmountable. My question is of a different nature: Do I have to undergo a complete change in personality to be a good trainer? It seems that most of the trainers I've seen have the same extroverted, jovial, outgoing kind of personality and that's not really "me." How can I maintain the essence of who I am while being an effective trainer?

Shy in Cheyenne

Dear Shy:

Yes, most trainers (particularly those who have *chosen* this profession) do seem to be outgoing and extroverted, but not all of them are. Granted, you will find more extroverts among those who get volunteered as trainers, but you'd be amazed at how many of us who stand before audiences have a shy side, too.

Most of us initially feel our shyness surfacing when we stand before a group. Accept that this is a normal occurrence. Getting angry or impatient with yourself for feeling stressed out will actually increase your discomfort. Simply consider the nervousness you feel as extra "energy" that will help you project your voice and punctuate your stance and gestures.

Second, do what you can to enjoy the process. Even if you tend to be shy, how do you like to have fun? Do you enjoy stories, cartoons, humorous anecdotes? Think about your unique way of expressing enjoyment and bring it with you to the classroom. Some of the most powerful speakers and trainers I've seen are, by nature, soft-spoken, introverted individuals. The secret is in being yourself, even if you have to speak a little louder than normal.

Third, remind yourself that there are two elements to every presentation: the presenter and the material. If you present strong material with good ideas that will benefit your learners, you'll feel your confidence grow. Just give yourself a chance, bring your full personality to the process, and expect to learn along with your learners. You'll be amazed at your progress!

Leslie

Dear Shy:

Don't forget that training sessions are filled with all kinds of people, many of whom are like you. Think of the relief quiet persons will feel when they realize that this session is being led by someone like them. The only thing I would suggest is that you watch your energy level. Sometimes people confuse energy with commitment—the higher the energy the higher the commitment to the subject at hand, the lower the energy the lower the commitment. You don't want people to misread your belief in your subject. Introverted presenters need to think in terms of intensity. You can be very effective by bringing a quiet intensity to the ideas you're sharing.

Chris

Dear Instant Trainers:

Our restaurant has begun a series of employee-led training sessions on safe food handling, service, innovative recipes, and cost-effective ordering strategies. I am one of the lucky people who get to talk on safe food handling and I want to look as confident and competent as possible. My mother says that regardless of who my audience may be, or what my topic is, posture is a big part of the presentation. Is she correct? If so, what do I need to know about posture and gestures?

Standing in South Bend

Dear Standing:

As always, your mother was right. Stance, posture, and gestures are important and you've come to the right place for a few instant secrets about this often overlooked topic. As for stance, "think straight lines." Stand straight (yet relaxed) with your weight evenly distributed on both feet. Flex your knees slightly (skiers know how to do this automatically). Keep your joints relaxed and this will keep you from looking rigid.

Consider that your energy begins in the soles of your feet, traveling up through your legs, through your trunk, and out to your audience. If you keep all of the lines straight, their energy bounces back to you. Here are two common pitfalls you'll want to avoid. Women sometimes break their straight lines by sinking onto one hip and leg. While it may look casual, it draws people's eyes from the face and onto the hip line. Men usually stand straight, but they often rock. Sometimes they rock side to side (rather than taking a step) and sometimes they rock front to back.

Avoid any repetitive behavior that might detract from your message. I once knew a speaker who did a "one, two, three step and bounce" movement so often audience members named it "The Dip." Obviously, that was too much. Think natural, be natural, while maintaining an upright stance.

The less you worry about "proper" gestures the better off you'll be. Just let your message drive what happens with your hands and arms. Don't worry about your hands and what to do with them; wherever your arms go so will your hands. Some trainers cross their arms or hold them in front of their bodies. That's okay, but it can be misread by the group. Try letting your arms hang loosely from your sides, and as you speak, just let your arms move naturally. You'll look more confident and credible.

Watch people's gestures, both in and out of the classroom. Compare fast, straight, punchy gestures with slower, softer, more rounded ones. Compare those who stand with relaxed arms (one or both hanging down) to those who stand with arms bent at the waist. What looks best to you? All gestures are not appropriate for all people and this is part of the practice of being yourself and doing what fits for you. If you allow your natural self to emerge, you'll stand head and shoulders above the rest.

Leslie

Dear Standing:

This is the perfect time for a "friend audit." Do you have a friend who cares for you enough to tell you the truth? If you do, you're a lucky person! Ask your friend the following question: Do I have any annoying gestures or habits that could be a distraction if I were in front of a group? When I asked that question, I learned that I had gotten into the habit of pushing my glasses up on my nose—often. I wasn't even aware that I did it. (I now wear contact lenses!) That is the kind of gesture you want to eliminate, and it will probably take someone else to call it to your attention.

Chris

 Dear Instant Trainers:

I've heard the old saw, "It isn't what you say, but how you say it." As a brand new trainer, I am wondering what I need to know about tone of voice and volume. Do I need to speak really loudly when I'm training? We've had a few trainers who have almost blown us out of the room with their volume, which seemed inappropriately loud for the size of the group. I am by nature a soft-spoken person, yet there have been times when I've had to strain to hear what a presenter said. I want to avoid either of these pitfalls and do whatever is appropriate for my group. What do I need to be aware of in this arena and how can you help me?

Auditory in Augusta

Dear Auditory:

Yes, voice tone and volume do make a difference, and in the beginning it's hard to know exactly what will best fit the occasion. Let's start with voice tone. Not all of us have the perfect speaking voice, but if we can keep our tone conversational, people will be more inclined to listen. Do not presume that you need to sound like an authority, nor come off as an expert. In fact, many participants resent a "teachy" or "preachy" tone, but if you express yourself in a conversational tone they will be more inclined to listen. Act as if you're simply presenting the ideas for consideration rather than telling people what they have to know.

You will be perceived as more credible if you end your sentences in a downward rather than upward intonation (save the upward for when you ask questions). For example, a trainer may say, "Consider trying this approach?" rather than "Consider trying this approach ..." And now consider which statement you'd find more convincing if you were a participant.

Regarding volume, in time you'll learn how to fit volume to the size of group. I'll assume you are speaking to smaller groups (35 or fewer) and that no microphone or amplification is necessary. Of course, for 35 people you will use a louder volume than for 10.

If you need to increase your volume, remind yourself that louder does not mean "up." Many people raise their tones upward when trying to increase volume and this can strain your voice. If you are naturally soft-spoken, start practicing small volume increases at home. Feel your voice bounce through the room and off the walls.

Some trainers, when asked to speak louder, do so; for one sentence, that is. Then they go back to their normal soft volume. If you need to project, do it consistently, without straining, of course!

If you need constant reminders to increase your volume, buy some fluorescent stickers and put them on your notes as reminders to speak up. Get feedback from your trainees on whether your volume is appropriate for the group size. Tape yourself occasionally, once you get used to the process, and judge for yourself. Indeed, what you say is often affected by how you say it, and with a little bit of experience you can adjust your volume and vocal variety to match the situation.

Leslie

Dear Auditory:

As long as you're thinking about your voice, let me add a suggestion: Think about how you breathe. Your ability to project your voice comfortably, over a longer period of time, is a direct result of your ability to breathe deeply. Try this: Inhale through your nose for the count of seven, hold your breath for two counts and then exhale through your mouth for seven counts. That's a deep breath! When we get nervous, we tend to breathe more quickly, in little short puffs that make our voices sound less confident and more nervous. Paying attention to your breathing will improve your voice, calm your nerves, and increase your thinking ability. What a combination!

Chris

Dear Instant Trainers:

I'm a brand new trainer who will be teaching territory management skills to our sales reps. Having spent several years on the road, I have the credibility to teach this topic, but one thing worries me. I don't know what to do about notes. I would like to organize my thoughts and have a written resource to rely on, but it seems that most of the trainers I've ever seen never seem to use notes. Am I wrong? Did they actually have notes but just hid them in some clever way? Please fill me in!

Noteless in Nacagdoches

Dear Noteless:

Most trainers use notes; even the experienced ones. Yes, there are clever ways to use notes that make them look invisible. The secret to working from notes is in creating key words or phrases that will remind you of a story, set of points, or key idea. Just like the seasoned trainers, you can glance at your material, catch the key word or phrase, and speak for several minutes on that one point.

- Keep in mind that a leader's guide is a big set of notes, or a series of them. Obviously, you need to familiarize yourself with the material ahead of time or you'd be reading to your group. Some trainers highlight the key points in their leader's guides so they will be sure to include them.

- Visual aids such as overhead transparencies, flip charts, and slides are the "invisible" notes many trainers use. Once you get your material organized and create your visual aids, you'll find that you, too, just like the trainers you've witnessed, can speak for a few minutes on one key point.

- If you have certain stories or anecdotes that illustrate points about territory management and you're worried about forgetting them, stick a Post-it note in your workbook, with a key word or phrase on it that will remind you about the story.

- Cartoons, quotations, or pictures can also work as visual cues for you to describe or demonstrate a key point.

The perceptions of participants are fascinating. I've conducted many trainings where people have said, "I can't believe you spoke to us all day and never used a note!" I smile and say "Thanks," glancing at the highlights in my workbook, my pile of transparencies, and notes I jotted down during the session. That's a noteworthy accomplishment if you ask me!

Leslie

Dear Noteless:

*One other tip. No matter what you use for your notes, 3 × 5 cards, a leader's guide, or overheads, **number them!** When they get knocked off the table or fly out of your hand after an exuberant gesture, having them numbered will save you time, not to mention embarrassment. Believe me, this one comes from personal experience.*

Chris

Chapter 18

HOW TO KNOW IF LEARNING HAS HAPPENED

Piglet sidled up to Pooh from behind. "Pooh," he whispered.
"Yes, Piglet."
"Nothing," said Piglet, taking Pooh's paw, "I just wanted to be sure of you."

Every trainer I know has felt like Piglet at one time. We watch the participants leave the training session, sometimes laughing, sometimes talking quietly, sometimes lingering for a little more conversation, sometimes rushing to get out of the room. The trainer stands in the front of the room, picking up overheads and taking the flip charts down from the walls, wondering, "Can I be sure anyone really learned anything?"

Tough question. Even more importantly, it's a dangerous question if not asked at the right time. Imagine a police department that does a training session on defusing the anger at the scene of a domestic abuse call or a manufacturing company that trains personnel on the proper procedure for the disposing of hazardous materials. They run the session, thank everyone for attending, and consider their job done. "Wait a minute," you say. "How do I know anyone actually learned the right stuff?" There could be serious consequences if we assume our learners learned and they didn't. Welcome to the world of training evaluation.

It's not enough for trainers to think they've done their job. Trainers need to prove that the knowledge and skills they've presented will be used at the job site. It's called transfer of learning and in this session you'll find ways to discover if it has happened. Some of these techniques are simple, many are more complex, but all of them are critical parts of the training process. If you care about the material that makes up your program, you'll need to find ways to evaluate your process.

Dear Instant Trainers:

In all my years of attending seminars, I am embarrassed to admit that I have never filled out an evaluation form because I didn't think they were all that important. Maybe it was the way the trainer asked, or just my own bad attitude, but I've always figured no one even read them! Well, last week I conducted my first two training sessions and although I asked my participants to fill out their evaluations, only about half of them did so. Now that I'm the one in the front of the room I can see where an evaluation can offer good feedback and let me know if my approach is on target. Is there any clever way I can coerce or persuade people to turn in their evaluations next time?

Contrite in Cleveland

Dear Contrite:

It's odd how we learn our lessons, isn't it? As someone who is fond of the evaluation process, I'm happy you've come around. And frankly, I'm surprised that only half of your group filled out their evaluations. Most people tend to comply with their presenter's request (my groups do). Did you make it a point to ask that the evaluations be completed? Were the forms just sitting there on the table along with everything else and were you expecting that people would fill them out without being asked? Did you draw attention to the form and let people know it was important?

Is the form long or complicated? Evaluation forms need to be convenient to complete. Four or five measurements are probably all you need to determine if you, your content, and the process of your session were effective. The criteria for a good evaluation can (and should) include:

- the trainer's effectiveness (delivery and responsiveness to the audience)

- the quality of the content and materials (practicality, relevancy, comprehensiveness)

- quality and effectiveness of audiovisuals (flip chart, transparencies, slides, props, support tools)

- use of games, role plays, simulations, or skill practice and their results

- the level of involvement on the part of the participants (a self-rating)

Try using a half-sheet for your evaluations. Some people are put off by having to fill out a whole page. Think ease and convenience. My favorite evaluation form combines forced choice and comments. It asks people to rate specific factors (content, delivery, activities, and self-evaluation) using either numbers (1 to 5) or evaluative words (excellent or outstanding to very good to okay or poor). I follow up the numerical or descriptive rating with the word "because" with space for comments. I want people to explain why they rated the program as they did. Incorporate the evaluation process as the "last official act" of your program. Be sure to leave time for it (an extra five to seven minutes will do).

Some trainers withhold a last handout or memento and exchange it for the evaluation. Others conduct a drawing, using the evaluations as the "tickets." Of course, this would mean people need to sign the form. You don't really need to be too clever or creative; simply communicate your desire for constructive feedback. Thank people ahead of time for their input and remember to give them time to complete the form. One last thought: Evaluate how you handle the evaluation process. You might come up with your own clever spin on this important aspect of training.

Leslie

Dear Contrite:

Willingness to fill out evaluation forms seems to be embedded in corporate culture. Some of my groups fill them out without being asked, some won't no matter how much I ask, and most are somewhere in between. First, I'd ask other people who do training in your organization what their response rates have been. If you discover that your people tend to ignore evaluation forms, I'd try a really simple one for a while. At the end of your training session, hand out an index card to each person and ask them to rate the session on a scale of 1 to 10 (one being the worst ever and 10 being the best session they've ever experienced).

Then ask them to answer two questions. Ask "What was the most helpful part of this session?" Pause to let them write, and then ask: "What would you change about this session?" Pause, and as you collect the cards, say "Thank you." Although this is not the best way to get feedback on your program, it will get you more than empty sheets of paper. After you've done this for a while and people come to see that you take their input seriously, you can move on to a more extensive evaluation.

Chris

Dear Instant Trainers:

Do I have to use evaluations in my programs? I mean, why should I want people to judge me? Isn't it enough for me to simply do my best and keep trying to improve? After all, what gives people the right to criticize everything I say and do? Please tell me it's okay to bypass the evaluation process.

Slippery in Salem

Dear Slippery:

We would slip up in our responsibilities as the Instant Trainers if we let you slide out on this one! Properly worded evaluations can function almost like a complete course on how to become an effective trainer. Yes, you will have your share of unusable comments, but with the proper attitude, you can slough off the innuendo and improve from the salient criticism.

For the most part, dismiss the general comments ("good," "bad") because they don't give you enough detail to duplicate or avoid whatever you did. People may comment on your appearance: Use your judgment on this one. Unless you receive incredibly consistent comments, you can probably dismiss most of the feedback regarding your personal taste in clothing.

But evaluation comments can offer you a crash course in self-improvement, so stay tuned in. People may tell you what worked, what didn't work, and what they liked best or least. They may tell you what they want more of, or less of, and they will also tell you things about yourself you may not know. For example, some trainers speak to the people on one side of the room more than the other. Other trainers constantly turn their backs on the audience and speak to the flip chart or board. Of course, you have to take the good with the bad, and maintain a positive attitude. Yes, some people will seemingly cut you to shreds, but for the most part their input can help you become an outstanding trainer who will stand a cut above the rest.

Leslie

Dear Slippery:

Reading evaluations can be as much fun as having a root canal done. Here's my best advice. Look for trends. If one person doesn't like my outfit, I ignore it, but if 20 percent of the class mentions my appearance, I'll go looking for feedback from some of my trusted colleagues. If three people in a ten-person class say they had a hard time following my directions, it's back to the drawing board. Feedback is often hard to take and most of us don't have much practice in dealing with it very well. Think of this part of the training process as a personal bonus. If you're willing to embrace the compliments and evaluate and act on the criticisms appropriately, you'll come out ahead!

Chris

 Dear Instant Trainers:

I just finished my first training session and right now I don't care if I ever do another one. After reading and rereading my evaluations I'm convinced that just about everyone hated my presentation. Okay, I'll admit there were a few nice comments, but that's not the point. The negative ones are a real problem! How can you help me never get negative evaluations again?

Crushed in Columbia

Dear Crushed:

The only way you can never get negative evaluations again is to never walk into a training room again, but that's not the point. And that's not the result we want. You see, you may become a trainer instantly, but there's really no such thing as a perfect instant trainer, or even a perfect trainer. There's always room for improvement. You mentioned being convinced that just about everyone hated your presentation, yet there were a few nice comments. There's more to feedback than meets the eye. In fact, you can find many positives in the negatives. A lot of this depends on your attitude.

Perhaps a Post-Session Analysis will help you put things in perspective:

First of all, what do you think you did right?

Are there any evaluation comments to support your perceptions?

What do you think were your mistakes?

Are there any evaluation comments to support these perceptions?

What are the recurring themes of the feedback?

What are the isolated comments (from only one person)?

If you were to objectively interpret the feedback you received, what were the major problems and how could they be corrected?

If you were preparing for this same presentation all over again, what would you do differently this time?

These and other searching questions can help you identify what you did right and what you need to do differently next time. Sometimes the comments that make us say "ouch" are so on target it's hard to admit. But if we can remove our defensiveness and remind ourselves that there's no such thing as instant success, we find the reserve to learn from those we teach!

Leslie

Dear Crushed:

I ran to one of my training buddies, Mike McKinley, with the same problem early in my career and he gave me some great suggestions. First, at the end of the session, pick up the evaluations and put them in a large envelope and seal it! Over the next 24 hours do your own mental evaluation. What made you happy about your session? What will you change for the next time? When were you at your best? What skills do you need to polish? Make a few notes to capture your ideas. Then, after you've done your own honest evaluation, open the envelope and read what the learners have said. Look for areas of agreement. Explore reasons your opinions differ. Absorb the compliments. Now you're ready to make an action plan to improve your next session.

Chris

 Dear Instant Trainers:

It's probably helpful for you to know right off that many of my coworkers think I'm an overachiever. I just think I'm conscientious. But enough of that; here's my question. As a new trainer, I know I will want to use participant evaluations so I can benefit from their feedback, but that's only part of the picture. I'd also like to know what kinds of tools, techniques, or strategies exist for me to evaluate myself. Any suggestions?

Self-Aware in St. Cloud

Dear Self-Aware:

Just asking the question means you will be tuned in to the process of fine-tuning your presentation. Evaluations are your first tool, because they offer you instant feedback. A post-session analysis is also helpful: five or six questions that help you identify what you did right and what you would do differently next time.

Consider also the benefits of audiotaping yourself. You can purchase a tape recorder small enough to fit on your belt, or even set one on your head table and let it roll. This will give you an opportunity to evaluate the entire session at your leisure. Videotaping is another option, although it requires finding someone to run the camera and the presence of a camera may inhibit your group somewhat. When you listen to or watch your presentation, be sure to identify what you're doing right because many of us (particularly perfectionists) have a tendency to look only for the flaws.

Another option is to invite an experienced trainer to sit in on your session so he or she can observe and evaluate you. Make sure this individual is skilled in the process, so you can receive a positive and objective appraisal. It is conscientious of you to ask about these tools, and any or all of these options will help you continue building your skills and improving yourself.

Leslie

Dear Self-Aware:

I'd like to emphasize Leslie's suggestion to ask someone to observe you. If you can find a training buddy and agree to sit in on at least parts of each other's sessions, you'll have a valuable source of feedback. Here's an idea to make your buddy system even more effective. Agree beforehand on what behaviors you want to work on. Focus your attention on specific areas. You might want to work on increasing participation and she might be interested in her vocal qualities. He might want to be a better question answerer and you might want to try some humor. No matter what the subject, you'll be able to help each other more when your observations are more specific than general.

Chris

Dear Instant Trainers:

Our company has a standard evaluation form that we're supposed to use after every training session. I may be crazy, but I don't think they tell us much more than whether or not people have a good time. How should training be evaluated?

Listening in Los Angeles

Dear Listening:

You've asked a critical question. End of the session evaluations usually don't measure much more than the learner's reaction to the package the training came in. They can tell you how good the facility was, and how people liked the food, room temperature, and meeting location. At the end of a session, you can find out about the process you took people through and how well you took them through it. What you can't discover is how well people will be able and willing to actually put what they've learned into practice.

You might think about evaluating twice rather than once. Continue to evaluate at the end of each session. Keep it simple and easy for people to respond. Look for trends in the feedback and make adjustments as you see ways to improve. Then add a follow-up evaluation. Again, make it short and simple (you're more likely to get a response) and ask people how they've used what they learned, what kind of results they're getting, and what didn't work as they expected it to. Use this feedback to review the content of your session. Reinforce those things people tell you are most valuable and rework the sections that don't get mentioned or don't seem to be working well in the real world.

A final hint: There are samples of both these forms of evaluation in Appendix E. Feel free to modify them to fit your needs.

Chris

Dear Listening:

Not all evaluations have to be on paper. Several years ago I worked with a group of school administrators who, after their meeting, went around the group and made oral comments about what had been done most effectively. It was also their practice to state what could have been done better, provided it was expressed in constructive terms. If you are conducting a series of sessions this would be a great way to make adjustments in your content and process as you go along.

One of the things I dislike about evaluations is what I think of as the privacy element. Watch how people fold their evaluation forms or place them face down. When feedback and comments are more forthcoming, I think everyone has made some strides in self-improvement. Imagine putting a series of three or four sentence-completion items on a flip chart or overhead and having people pick a sentence or two to finish on the spot, or having small groups tackle each item and then give a report. Like anything else in the classroom, there are many ways to give feedback. You might try some of these if you find the standard evaluation form process wearying.

Leslie

Dear Instant Trainers:

When I was first asked to do some training in our bookstore I was flattered and terrified. After I did the program a few times, I felt comfortable and proud. Now that I'm ready to add "trainer" to my resume, I'm concerned. What if we're all having a good time and no one's learning anything? How can you measure the effects of your training efforts?

Muddled in Madison

Dear Muddled:

Turn back a page or two and read what Listening in Los Angeles asked. See, you're not alone. Let me add one thing to my answer to Listening's question. There is a wonderful book that really explores the whole issue of evaluating training, titled *Evaluating Training Programs: The Four Levels,* by Donald Kirkpatrick. If you want to delve deeper into the evaluation process this book is the best place to start. Some of what Kirkpatrick says may be out of reach for the training you do, but learning about evaluation at the four possible levels will make you a better trainer.

Chris

Dear Muddled:

As with Listening's situation, a series of take-back-to-the-job follow-up evaluations would fit the bill. You could ask people what they are doing differently; what they're more aware of; what behaviors or attitudes have changed. One question a week would give you a systematic format for ongoing self-improvement.

Leslie

Dear Instant Trainers:

I have a question that I've been thinking about for a while. Is the trainer the only person whose actions should be evaluated? I think it might be helpful for the participants to evaluate their own efforts. Do you agree? If so, how could you accomplish this kind of evaluation?

Self-Evaluated in St. Louis

Dear Self-Evaluated:

Seems only fair, doesn't it? If the trainees get to tell you how you did, they should own their level of participation. I agree.

At the beginning of a session, you can let people know that they will be asked to complete an evaluation form at the end of the session (some trainers pass the forms out at the beginning of the session so people can record comments during the session) and let them know that they'll be asked to rate their own participation. I think it's only fair to point out this question on the evaluation because very few trainers ask it.

When you review the evaluations, you'll probably see a connection between the way participants evaluated themselves and the way they rated you. This makes sense, because most of us respond positively to a highly energetic group and have a more difficult time with a nonparticipative audience. If your rating is consistently lower than the group rates itself, ask a trusted colleague to observe your next session and give you feedback. If you're getting ratings consistently higher than the group is rating itself, you may need to review your material. It's hard for trainees to participate if they don't feel as if the content applies in their world.

The good news is that any evaluation gives you new information to use as you work to make your sessions better. Good luck.

Chris

Dear Self-Evaluated:

Here's a good question you could ask participants in a sentence-completion format: "I could have gotten more out of this training if I…." I suspect you would get a totally different answer if you eliminated the personal pronoun at the end of the sentence. This helps participants take responsibility for their learning and it also gives you some insights into their attitudes. You see, some people may still try to put the responsibility on you. Those are the types who would write, "If I'd had a better instructor …" or "If I had been able to under-stand what the trainer was saying…." Reading self-evaluative comments is an education in itself!

Leslie

Chapter 19

DEVELOPING SUPPORT MATERIALS

If you write it, they will learn.

line cut from the final print of Field of Dreams

Imagine a workplace where there was one full-time trainer for each work team. This trainer's job would consist of being available 24 hours a day to answer questions, remind people to use their techniques and skills, provide feedback, and, when necessary, step in and perform the task. No one would need to take notes in class, carry a checklist back to the office, or participate in an assessment exercise. The trainer would be an immediate reference resource for each employee.

Sound like any workplace you've ever known? We doubt it. If the participants in your training sessions had access to you all the time there would be no need for you to develop training support materials. But they don't, so you should.

The question then becomes not "Do I need training support materials?" but "What kind of support materials do I need to prepare?" The best are materials that people keep and actually use! We've seen participants on planes lugging home a two-inch thick binder with the sneaking suspicion that they'll never actually look inside it again. The binder will have a place of honor on a shelf until it is replaced by the next binder—from the next training session. We both live in paper-producing states and like to support our local industries, but we're also quite fond of trees and would prefer that they be cut down for a worthy reason.

Effective training support materials consist of handouts that cause the trainee to take notes, workbooks that become a ready resource of helpful ideas and processes, and well-designed job aids that help participants practice what they've learned back in the real world, on the job. Trainers who become masters of support materials add value for their customers, the trainees. These trainers ensure that the impact of their sessions lasts beyond the doors of the classroom. Their materials become a ready resource for their trainees.

Dear Instant Trainers:

I can't decide if I've never used a handout for the software training session I do for our new customer service reps because I want to save a tree or because I have no idea what would make a handout useful. Are there any guidelines for creating and using handouts?

Careful in Corpus Christi

Dear Careful:

The trees of the world thank you for your concern, and we're all using recycled paper, aren't we? Handouts should be worth the paper they're printed on. Here's what will make them worthy.

- **Handouts need to be usable.**
  A handout that is usable encourages note taking (has sufficient white space for writing), is easy to read (is not a fifth-generation copy of someone else's handout on the subject), and is tied to the presentation (follows the same pattern as the presentation).

- **Handouts need to be keepable.**
  Multiple-page handouts that are hole-punched in a binder for a longer session or spiral bound for a shorter session are more apt to be kept. Of course, handouts that cover important and well thought-out content will be kept, binder or not!

- **Handouts need to be attractive.**
  With the availability of desktop publishing, a piece of paper that looks as if it was created on an IBM Selectric won't get much attention. Even a simple word processing package will allow you to lay out an interesting page.

Providing a copy of your overheads or slides isn't, by itself, a great handout. Look through the notes you have kept from some of the programs you've attended and see what worked for you. You'll get some good ideas and have a chance to review some of your notes. What a bonus, you might rediscover something important!

Chris

Dear Careful:

Here are a couple of additional thoughts about helpful handouts. Use an attention-getting font for a header so right away, when the owner of this document looks at it, the sheet will be easy to recognize and remember. You can easily add visual interest with an attractive border across the top, or a cartoon or image of some sort.

Attractiveness includes visual balance. Chris mentioned the importance of white space, not just for writing, but for contrast, too. Make sure your print is large enough to read. A full page of 10 point type (or smaller) with no margins and little space between sections will put off today's busy professionals (not to mention tiring aging eyes!). Challenge yourself to make your point clear and use as few words as possible. That's what Chris and I used as our goal for The Instant Trainer. I hope you think we succeeded!

Leslie

 Dear Instant Trainers:

I overheard two trainers talking and it sounded like the trainer who had a workbook thought her program was better because the other trainer only had handouts. What's the difference between a handout and a work-book? Should I care?

Eavesdropping in Evansville

Dear Eavesdropping:

Overheard conversations are often the best, aren't they? The difference between handouts and workbooks is usually a function of how they're packaged and how many pages they include. I think the reason you should care is that you care for your participants.

If you have lots of papers to hand out, don't staple them in the corner and hope that that will make them user friendly. The papers start to tear, it's hard to write, and the learner is annoyed. How much better to hole-punch them and put them in a binder. Even if you don't want to give the participants all the pages at once, you can start with the binder and dole out the pages as you go along. If you don't mind everything being given out at once, you might consider doing spiral binding—it's usually cheaper than a binder and will lie flat for note taking. On the other hand, don't put a few pages in a binder just to make your materials look impressive. It won't work!

The trainers you overheard were measuring the wrong thing. Length doesn't tell you anything about quality. Check out our answer to Careful in Corpus Christi earlier in this chapter for some ideas about useful handouts. Be sure to write us again when you overhear another conversation!

Chris

Dear Eavesdropping:

Chris is right. You create learning materials with your learners in mind, not your peers. Sometimes it's easy to think that what we do or how we do it is the right way or the only way. Some of the considerations you'll use for deciding whether you want to create a workbook or a small set of handouts are: budget, length of session, potential shelf life of the material, and how the materials will be used after the program.

Sometimes you have to do the best you can with what you have. Many of my clients create stapled sets for their employees; while I think three-hole punched sheets in a binder are great, they just don't have the budget for such items. We often spiral bind our workbooks for clients, but those cost money, too, and so are not always an option. I try to be flexible and accommodate the needs of my clients. Sometimes that means creating only a couple of work-

sheets or going with the bargain basement option of papers stapled together.
Even though the stapled sets are not the classiest in the world, some of my for-
mer participants tell me they still have, and still use, some of mine from a
decade ago. From my perspective, I'd rather my participants have humble
handouts that add value than none at all!

Leslie

 Dear Instant Trainers:

At the last training session I attended I noticed that the handouts were
printed on colored paper. Either the trainer got a special deal at Kinkos or
there was a reason for using color. My handouts are all on white paper. Am I
missing something?

Colorblind in Cortez

Dear Colorblind:

Maybe they did get a deal from their local copy center, but I'd guess
they used the colored paper for a reason. Try this experiment. Take three
pieces of white paper and three pieces of a brightly colored paper and put
each stack on a table. Look at the table from a distance and note your reaction. If you walked into the room, at which place would you sit? Now imagine one room with all white paper handouts and another with the handouts
on the colored sheets. If the same class was being given in each room and
you could choose which one you'd rather attend, what would you decide? I
bet you'd go for the colored paper both times. Why?

The colored paper engages the right side of your brain and suggests
that this session is going to be more fun. Because you've encouraged participation from the less-used (in today's business world) right side of the brain,
people who attend your class do so with their whole brains. Just think, all
that for a few pennies more!

Chris

Dear Colorblind:

Because most of my programs involve multiple pages (workbooks rather
than single handouts) I still use white paper for content pages, but I always
use colored paper for the covers. The colors range from a bright single color to

multicolored and they are attention-getting on two counts: the colors I use and the elaborate visuals on the cover. I agree with Chris about the use of color and consider it value added. When handing out single sheets or supplemental information, I like to save the best and the brightest colors for afternoon, when people's energy levels are beginning to drop. The category of "laser colors" are the best for this purpose.

Here's another consideration. How often have you almost ruined your eyesight rummaging through a file, trying to find a particular piece of paper? Imagine how much easier it might be if that piece of paper were a riveting blue, rocketing red, or shocking pink. Color not only helps gain attention on the spot, but it can help you retrieve a document later (think of all of the color-coded files you've seen in physician's and dentist's offices). Once you break out the colors, you'll never go back to using only white: You'll want handouts that are standouts!

Leslie

Dear Instant Trainers:

Do you think people will assume I'm belittling them if I use some of the clip art I've found in my word processing program? Some of the pictures are fun and would fit in the program I've been asked to put together on dealing with upset customers. There's one cartoon of a guy who looks as if he might explode that would be perfect.

Pictureless in Peoria

Dear Pictureless:

Go for it! The expression, "A picture's worth a thousand words," applies to clip art as well as photographs. I love sprinkling pictures throughout my handouts, but never more than one on a page. As you choose the clip art you want to use, you might want to keep a few things in mind.

- Choose a style of clip art and stick with it throughout a program. If you chose a cartoon for your first clip art addition, don't use representational art on the next page. Using several styles of clip art in a document is like using too many fonts on a page. It looks unprofessional.

- Consider coordinating the clip art you use on your slides or overheads with the clip art you use on your handouts. If the picture on the overhead matches the one next to the place you want people to take notes about the concept, you've done a good job reinforcing your message.

- The clip art that comes with a word processing program or presentation software is so widely used, you're apt to see "your" picture in another trainer's workbook. Check out the computer catalog that I'm sure you get weekly for some clip art collections (check out the suggestions in Appendix C). They're inexpensive and if you have access to a CD-ROM drive, you can get more clip art than you'll ever need on one CD.

Chris

Dear Pictureless:

Cartoons and visual images enhance your verbal message. I love my Click Art Cartoon CDs and use them all the time. Chris mentioned only using one image per page, but I take a different tack and use more. Let's say I feature three main points on a particular workbook page. I may use a small cartoon image to reflect each point. There's lots of white space, good visual balance, and enough separation between each written item and image that the page doesn't look crowded. I've received enough positive feedback from my participants that it would be hard to dissuade me from this practice.

Perhaps this is one of those areas that takes trial and error. Or it might depend on how much artistic ability you have. I don't mean the kind of artistic talent to draw the cartoon characters, but the kind of talent to recognize balance and style. If you have that, you may be able to "break the rules" and be a little more excessive.

Most of the time I use my cartoon images to contrast with my written message. That is, if one of my statements is about self-confidence, there's an image of a scaredy cat (an actual cartoon of a cat) next to it. Or if I'm talking about being organized, I'd use a cartoon of someone buried in massive piles of paper. Maybe matching the text with the cartoon allows me to get away with using so many. It's an easy way to introduce a subtle element of humor into your programs, and the fun part is that most people get it. In short, visuals send a variety of messages about you and it's nice to cover so many levels of communication at once.

Leslie

Dear Instant Trainers:

I have a sneaking suspicion that the handouts I so carefully prepare end up in a wastebasket a respectful distance from our meeting room. Do you know how to prepare handouts that are so helpful that people actually keep them and refer to them after the training?

Puzzled in Portsmouth

Dear Puzzled:

I think what you're looking for is called a *job aid.* To me, a job aid is a brief synopsis of a procedure or a process, or a checklist that a trainee would need to to remember in a hurry. Here's when an 8 1/2 × 11 piece of paper isn't your best choice.

Try thinking of ways you could put the key points of your material (e.g., ten characteristics of a high-performance team) or the steps of a process (e.g., the five steps to dealing with an upset customer) on a business card or index card size, heavier weight paper and have them laminated. These are the kinds of handouts people keep.

Another suggestion is to make developing a checklist or a job aid a class project. It would be a good review at the end of a section or session, you could produce them and distribute them after the session as a follow-up reminder, and you'd get some good examples to use with other groups.

Chris

Dear Puzzled:

If you have some information you want to make sure people hang onto, and it needs to go on a standard size piece of paper, you can also experiment with different paper stocks. Certificate paper, for example, which will run thought any laser printer or copier, can make a document look official. Or buy some fancy paper with a colored border, or paper that showcases a special image (flowers, a tree, a sunset, the ocean, rainbows, clouds, etc.). I use these special papers all the time, and it's fun to walk into someone's office and see my work on the wall or in a frame on the desk.

Going back to Chris' approach of using odd sizes of paper, there's also the option of creating oversized bookmarks on which to put your inspirational or educational content. Suffice it to say, if you want people to hang onto your message over time, make it worth their while to do so.

Leslie

Chapter 20

USING AUDIOVISUALS TO IMPROVE YOUR PRESENTATION

People don't learn by words alone!

Preparing for a training session takes more than deciding what to say. Effective trainers recognize that people learn better when more of their senses are involved in the process. Using audiovisuals, from a low-tech flip chart to high-tech computer-generated images, can add excitement, interest, and retention to your training session.

They can also add a layer of anxiety, complexity, and unpredictability to your session. Any trainer can tell you an audiovisual horror story. Bulbs burn out in both overhead and slide projectors. Computer cables may plug in on one end but not match on the other. Even a simple flip chart can wobble, collapse, and refuse to let go of a page. We've all lived through these experiences. The lighting is dim, the trainer pushes a button, there's a sudden flash of light, and the room plunges into darkness. Or the projector goes on and an unreadable overhead fills the screen. The trainer says, "I know you can't read this but...."

So, you ask, "What's a trainer to do? Abandon AV and go back to straight talk?" No, far from it! 3M has done research that reinforces what trainers have always known: Audiovisuals significantly increase retention of material by the learner and are well worth the effort expended by the trainer. That's the key—effort by the trainer. You can produce visuals that reinforce your messages effectively when you learn how to develop visuals that people can see, read, and remember. You can avoid most of the common AV disasters if you take the time to prepare and practice. You can deal with the unexpected problems with style and grace when you understand the working of the equipment you're using and have a back-up plan. Using audiovisuals requires that you, the trainer, become the learner.

Dear Instant Trainers:

Our bank has introduced a major culture change and I get to lead the training initiative for transforming our tellers from primarily service providers to salespeople. We have purchased an impressive training package and I get to facilitate it. The program is designed around a series of videos which participants will be required to watch as a group. I do have some concerns about people staying focused on the content as each video is 45 minutes long. So tell me, Instant Trainers, are my concerns valid? I am wondering how I can keep people interested over that period of time so we can make the most of all the money we invested in this series. What do you suggest?

Validated in Venice

Dear Validated:

Yes, it is tough keeping people focused on movies or videos, especially when they exceed 20 minutes in length. People often tap out while watching a training film or video. This may be a result of television viewing, which is a passive activity. Here are some strategies to keep people focused and alert while viewing your videos:

1. Assign tasks that must be done during the video. Instruct your tellers to look for a certain segment and observe it carefully. Have them note how many times a word or concept comes up.

2. Play "stop and go." After a significant scene or vignette, stop the tape and ask how the situation might have been handled differently, or what suggestions anyone has for improving the situation.

3. Create a worksheet to accompany the video if one doesn't already exist. Design it in such a way that it's interactive: People have to write things down, keep track of something, or add their own comments to coincide with what they see or hear on the video.

4. Develop a list of post-viewing questions that will encourage a discussion of the major points in the video.

5. Find a logical stopping place in the middle of the 45 minutes. Engage in a spirited discussion, take a quick break, role play, or engage in some other kind of activity before people view the second half.

6. Play off people's competitive nature and ask them to organize into teams and find out who can come up with the longest list of positive or negative examples (it's up to you) where people in the video sold supremely well or washed out.

Giving people a varied format such as in the examples above keeps them more alert and active, and avoids fatigue or distraction. You want to do whatever you can to ensure your trainees are internalizing the message. Let everyone know they can expect to be called on once the video ends; it encourages them to pay more attention and holds them accountable for what they observed. Your role as a change agent will require patience, creativity, and a gentle firmness. Let your tellers know you expect them to take an active part in the training so they can act on what they learn. A valid premise of effective sales training, if you ask me!

Leslie

Dear Validated:

I was in the same situation you're facing and was bound by the rules of the course to play the video from beginning to end. Imagine my concern when, during the first session, I watched people nodding off after 20 minutes. Here's what I did for subsequent sessions: made popcorn. At the 20-minute mark, I quietly left the room, went to the lunch room, and popped three bags of microwave popcorn. When I returned 10 minutes later, the smell alone brought everyone to attention. We munched for the balance of the video and had a lively discussion when it was over. Sometimes you just have to get creative!

Chris

Dear Instant Trainers:

Imagine yourself just minutes from starting your program. Instead of your slide carousel fitting smoothly into the projector, it crashes to the floor and all the slides fall out. I don't have to imagine—it happened to me! Can you give me some hints so my next experience with slides will be more peaceful?

Embarrassed in Elkhorn

Dear Embarrassed:

If anything can go wrong with audiovisual equipment, it will, so plan for the unexpected, bring your sense of humor, and use a little common sense. The best thing you can do when you use any equipment is to set your room up in plenty of time so you can take care of any of these glitches before people arrive. If, for some good reason, you can't do things beforehand and the worst happens in front of an audience, be prepared to be a good sport about it. If you get upset or rattled, the group will respond to your discomfort. If you can laugh, the group will too. Common sense needs to be packed in every trainer's toolkit. Number your slides (overheads, too) so you can get them back in order quickly. I can't promise the slide carousel will never fall again, but if it does you'll be better prepared.

Since you asked about slides, I can offer a few other hints to make the slides you show more effective. Katie Weiser, Global Director of Education for Deloitte & Touche Consulting Group, has written a great article about making your visuals more effective. She has given me permission to share three of her best hints:

The purpose of slide text is to highlight *key points*. Often presenters cram most of their mateial on the slide and read from it—a terrific crutch resulting in boring presentations. Slides should have no more than six lines of text and use a type font that is clearly readable from the back of the room.

Background colors for large-screen presentations should always be dark, the opposite of what we would generally see on a printed page. Black backgrounds allow information to "float" on the screen with no discernable border. Dark, low-energy backgrounds with bright, high-energy graphics and white and yellow text will always be the easiest to use.

The choice of slide mounts is a no-brainer—always select glass, never cardboard or plastic. Glass mounts prevent visuals from "popping" in and out of focus as the projection lamp heats the chip of film in the slide projector. They also keep unwanted fingerprints off your important information.

Just one more thought from my experience. Every time I venture into a new technology, I go to school to learn all I can about the equipment I'll be using. Going to school in this case means finding a vendor in my community who will spend time coaching me on the ins and outs of what I need know and letting me practice to my heart's content. If you work in a large organization, you might be able to find an expert to coach you in your own building. Either way, take the time to learn. A day will come when you'll be glad you did!

Chris

Dear Embarrassed:

I used to work in a media library, and learned a couple of things about working with slides. The technology has improved since then, but the basic design is still the same. First of all, always make sure the tray retainer ring on the top of your slide tray is screwed on tightly. This way, even if you drop your slide carousel your slides will stay intact.

My other tip is to avoid leaving an image on the screen after you're finished explaining it. People will tend to look at an image on the screen regardless of its relevance. So show your slide, explain it, and be done with it; this way the focus will come back to you.

Last, keep the room lights as bright as possible while showing your slides so people don't snooze out on you. Get comfortable using a remote and you'll have a show worth watching!

Leslie

Dear Instant Trainers:

Ever since I ordered a book on training I've been getting a new catalog of training supplies almost daily. Many of them advertise videos to use with a training program. I thought a video could be an interesting way for us to learn more about conflict. We're a small store so we don't have much to spend on training and many of the videos are quite expensive. Are videos a good way for adults to learn?

Cost Conscious in Chicago

Dear Cost Conscious:

Videos are a natural addition to a training session—TV viewing has become a way of life for most people. Videos also provide access to material and speakers that smaller organizations could never afford. But (and it's a big **but**) putting people into a room, turning on a TV, and asking them to watch isn't training! There are two ways you can maximize your training dollars: **preview** and **rent.**

Most training videos are available for your review on a preview basis. When you find a video you're interested in, call and ask for their preview policy. Before you spend any money, preview the video. A video you want all your current and new employees to see is a video you'll want to buy. A video you think might be helpful to a smaller group of employees or that you'd only show one time is one to rent. It doesn't make sense to rent a video over and over nor does it make sense to buy a video you'll only use once.

Pull a few of those training catalogs out of the trash and look again. There just might be a video that will fit into your training plan very well.

Chris

Dear Cost Conscious:

Chris hit upon two important considerations and I'll reiterate in case you didn't catch them. Preview is essential. You want to avoid shocking yourself or your employees with a surprise ending or an element that goes counter to your culture or practices (for example, a few training videos allow vernacular, including a few swear words, while others are extremely dated and may have sexist language or no ethnic diversity). There are enough video companies and vendors out there to choose from so you can find exactly what you want.

Again, usage will determine whether you rent or purchase. As a small company, you would find rental most appealing unless the video is such an epic you'll play and replay it (this I seriously doubt).

Look for hidden resources. For example, universities, community colleges, and sometimes Intermediate School Districts (otherwise known as Regional Educational Service Agencies) may have libraries of training films available to local businesses for a low rental fee. Also check Chambers of Commerce, Small Business Assistance offices, and even the training departments of state agencies (Civil Service, for example, which is often the service agency to all other departments within a state). Last but not least, if you or anyone else in your company belong to trade or professional associations, check out their libraries, too. Included in that list of associations, of course, would be the local chapter of the American Society for Training and Development. If you're not a member, contact someone who is, because every now and then, local chapters sponsor film festivals. They're quite handy events: one-stop resources where you can preview the latest and the best training films on the market for an approachable one-day registration fee. These are among my favorite ASTD events and I wish our local chapter held one every year. The video you want may be available at a fraction of what it would cost you to buy or even rent, so it will pay you to check out every available local option before you lay down your company's hard-earned cash.

Leslie

Dear Instant Trainers:

When I heard the words *computer-based training* my heart just about stopped. I still secretly believe that if I hit the wrong button on my computer, the company will cease to exist. If I hate computers, will I loathe CBT? How can a computer program be better than a live, warm-blooded trainer?

Technoless in Tulsa

Dear Technoless:

You've fallen into the trap of trainer versus computer. Get out of it! From the beginning of time most of us have resisted things that are new, unfamiliar, and different. CBT is today's version of the overhead projector of years ago—another tool for trainers to use. The real issue isn't whether CBT is good, it's when it should be used. Leslie and I could have written this book completely by fax, E-mail, and direct computer connection. Although we used all these high-tech tools, we still chose to find ways to work person to person, tackling those issues that required face-to-face conversation. Training should be looked at in the same way.

Much training that can be captured in a CBT program works wonderfully. Students can access the material at times that fit their schedules. They can move at their own pace and (probably most importantly) they can review all or parts of the program as many times as they need to in order to insure a good grasp of the material. On the other hand, training that involves discussion and give and take needs to happen in groups with a well-prepared trainer as the participants' guide.

I don't think computer-based training will ever replace good trainers, as long as trainers keep working on being good!

Chris

Dear Technoless:

Imagine a world in which learners can be self-directed. They can create their own schedules, control their own learning curves, and pace their learning. They can also consult with an expert when they have a question or need encouragement. In other words, with the right attitude and approach, you can offer your learners the best of both worlds.

I like to think that in-person training *will never go out of style. But it's exciting to employ the latest in technology for education, and you have that opportunity through CBT. Chris and I both think that, with a positive approach, in a few months we'll hear you say, "CBT is the way for me!" We look forward to your announcement!*

Leslie

 Dear Instant Trainers:

Our department consists of salespeople who make, on average, three presentations per week. The boss went to an industry meeting and fell in love with Microsoft's Power Point presentation software and decided since we all had laptops, we could easily do computer-based presentations. Guess who got the job of figuring out how to make the software and the equipment work? Since I'm supposed to share my learning with my peers who are as confused as I am, can you help?

Pointless in Port Edwards

Dear Pointless:

Computer-generated presentations are about the hottest things around these days. Here's the good news: The people who are developing these packages seem to have figured out that the majority of people who use them are not computer whizzes, so they have made the programs pretty easy to learn.

That is, of course, if you're not trying to use one for the first time the night before you have to give the presentation! This is a perfect example of when playing is the best way to learn. Most of the programs come with either a built-in tutorial or one included in the manual. Go through it. Read the manual. Go to your local bookstore and buy a support book for the program. Play around with a presentation in different formats. Learn how to produce overheads and slides. Find a format for handouts that you like. Don't overlook the speaker's notes functions. Do all this without a presentation deadline. If you start out working under pressure, you'll learn enough to survive and never go back and take the time to really learn all that you could. (By the way, all of this won't take you very long. These programs are amazingly simple and fun to work with.) Then prepare and give a presentation—probably about using the presentation software you're using—and see how it goes. You'll have added a valuable skill.

If you're going to run your presentation off the computer, the equipment is another story. This can be tricky if you're hooking up to unfamiliar equipment or have a cranky computer. One of my very techno-literate friends says he always carries a set of overheads as backup just in case the computer crashes or he runs into a connection problem. Good advice for you to keep in mind. If you all have laptops, you must have a vendor who views your organization as a good customer. Now's the time to ask for their expertise. Find out what other equipment you'll need, how to do setup under all kinds of circumstances, and have the vendor help you practice.

Remember the first time you had to write on a flip chart and you couldn't figure out where to stand, how large to write, and what color pen to use for best visibility? This really is the same thing, only with cords, computers, and big screens. Eventually it won't feel like a big deal!

Chris

Dear Pointless:

Maybe you can take comfort in knowing that I am not a technological whiz, but I found learning my presentation software package extremely fun and only a little bit intimidating. Within four hours I was able to put together my first computer-generated slide presentation, complete with fades. As Chris said, it takes a bit of reading and the willingness to start playing.

Once you learn the basics of the package you can start stretching its limits. I enjoy working with overheads, so my application needs are limited. So I decided to push my limits in other areas. I learned how to import clip art images from CDs into Power Point so my visuals wouldn't look like everyone else's. I also learned how to recolor images that came along with Power Point, after deciding they didn't provide me with as diverse a population of business-people as I'd hoped. While I can't change the ages of the people featured in the software, I can change their appearance.

The bottom line: If you have a sense of balance and any kind of design ability, you'll find yourself having fun with your presentation software package. And isn't having fun part of the point?

Leslie

 Dear Instant Trainers:

I love music, all kinds—from country to classical. I'd like to bring my love of music to my training sessions. I know it would put me in a good mood to hear a little Mozart or to hum some Golden Oldies, but would anyone else benefit? What do you think about music during a training session?

Melodious in Memphis

Dear Melodious:

Music, well placed, can enhance a training session. There are two things to consider: Is it the right music in the right place, and do you have the proper permission to use it?

Let's consider the last issue first. Copyrighted music that is played in public places for other than the purchaser's private use (e.g., stores, restaurants, and hotel meeting rooms) is subject to licensing fees that are paid to ASCAP or BMI. Check to see if your organization pays those royalties. If the answer is yes, turn on the CD player. If the answer is no, you'll need to look for music that extends the rights that allow you to play it for more than personal enjoyment. Here are two possibilities. Call Creative Training Techniques at 1-800-383-9210 and ask for their catalog. In it you will find a tape that is especially designed for use in the training room. While you're dialing, call the people at OptimaLearning, 1-800-672-1717, and ask about their specially selected and sequenced Baroque and Other Classical Music for Learning series. They extend permission to use their tapes in corporate classrooms and meeting rooms.

Now to musical choice. I love to have music playing when people enter the meeting room. If the session is early in the morning, I usually choose something calmly classical, after lunch something more up-tempo. If you don't have to worry about licensing and your session lasts over a longer time period, you can ask your participants to bring in some of their favorite tunes.

One other time to think music is during work sessions. The Optima-Learning tapes are perfect for this use. Read the instructions that come with the tapes and you'll learn that the proper use of the right music will hasten comprehension, increase retention of any information, and enhance motivation of the learner.

Thanks for this question. It reminded me to get up and turn on my CD player.

Chris

Dear Melodious:

I used to love playing New Age music on my boom box at my training sessions until I discovered I was violating copyright laws. However, I did learn a few things about music in the classroom during that period and I'd love to share them. Instrumentals are far superior to vocal music. In fact, the reason I liked New Age music is that it's low-key and when you shut it off people aren't still singing the songs or tapping their toes (as they would be if you were playing vocal music).

In the days when I played music in my training sessions, people told me they felt more comfortable coming into the room; many told me it was easy to speak to someone else (even a stranger) because there was noise in the room and their voices didn't break the silence. I also used it as a signal during breaks. When the music stopped, the group knew it was time to begin again.

In addition to Creative Training Techniques, there are music houses that sell public domain music. But I have a cousin who is a classical guitarist and your question has encouraged me to commission him to make some tapes just for me—of his original works. This way I can play music that appeals to me aesthetically and once again create the ambience I once had and so sorely miss.

Leslie

Dear Instant Trainers:

I've been elected to present a series of brief updates on our safety program and my manager keeps telling me to keep it simple. Yet, one element I've always enjoyed as a trainee is the visual aspect. I don't want to be just a talking head, but I also have no budget for this project. I did notice, in the storage closet next to the training room, an old flip chart and easel stand, and I even found a few colored markers and an ancient overhead projector. The projector fan is terribly loud so I'm not sure I want to use it, but the flip chart looks promising. However, I'm long on enthusiasm but short on artistic talent. Can you help me?

Artsy in Anchorage

Dear Artsy:

While a flip chart would not be considered the latest technological breakthrough in visual aids, this old standard can add a dash of color to your safety training.

Here are two strategies for the unartistic person's approach to producing a flip chart:

1. Find someone in your office who possesses artistic ability and ask this talented individual what it would take to produce a series of colorful pages on your flip chart. Often, people who can print and draw well enjoy this kind of work so much they are more than willing to help out. If that is not the case, resort to strategy number two, which falls under the category of working smarter, not harder.

2. Find a young child's activity book or coloring book. With safety as your topic, you might find some cute or humorous illustrations that would go along with your material. Make a copy of this page on your office copier (surely you have one, right?) using transparency stock. Most copy machines today will run transparencies with no problem. Take that old overhead projector, put the transparency on it, and project it on the flip chart. Trace the image onto the paper (or ask your talented coworker to do this), using whatever colors are available, and pretty soon, you'll have a classy-looking flip chart. Remember to leave a blank sheet in between the sheets you draw on so the images don't bleed through. You can tape the drawn page and blank sheet together if you like for ease of use. This way, you can present your program with just a little bit of pizzazz!

Leslie

Dear Artsy:

Leslie and I must have wanted to spend more time in kindergarten. She's into coloring books and I'm into cut and paste! Here's one more idea to try. Grab some of those old magazines in your reception area, a pair of scissors, and a glue stick. Cut out some pictures that match your topic and use them on your flip charts. Just make sure you cut out pictures that are big enough for people to see from the back of the room. These pictures will add color and interest to your program. Some of them might turn out so well you'll want to hang them on the walls for other programs.

Chris

Dear Instant Trainers:

Is anybody still using a flip chart as a support tool in presentations? In this day and age of high-tech training, flip charts seem so low-tech. Will I lose my credibility and be laughed out of the room?

Flipped Out in Fond du Lac

Dear Flipped Out:

You can take comfort in the fact that low-tech is still alive and well on the training track. You don't need portable electronics, patch cords, and high-tech paraphernalia to be an Instant Trainer. You can still dazzle your devotees and present your ideas effectively with the flick of your wrist. Part of what makes flip charts good training tools is their low cost, portability, versatility, and ease of use. Flip charts can be used in meetings, training programs, informative presentations, and a variety of other situations. In a classroom, maximum class size for flip chart use is approximately 30 to 35 people. You can prepare a chart pad ahead of time and use two flip charts, one with prepared information, charts, or colorful illustrations, and the other to use as you would a chalk board.

Some pads come in newsprint but they don't look as crisp as the higher quality stock. If you are preparing your flip chart ahead of time, keep at least one blank sheet between pages to avoid marker bleed-through. This will also prevent people from being able to read what is written on the next page before you get there. If the chart paper is thin, you may have to use as many as three sheets. To hold sheets together (which keeps you from having to count sheets every time you turn a page) fasten them on the bottom right and left sides with white mailing labels.

If you are one of those individuals who cannot write in a straight line, you can purchase easel pads with light blue horizontal (ruled) lines or a combination of horizontal and vertical lines over the entire surface (grid style). If all else fails, draw your own lines on each sheet, providing you know how to handle a ruler and draw light lines with a pencil.

Use bold, dark, readable colors and avoid light colors such as orange, yellow, or pink. Use fluorescent colors for highlighting or underlining only. If the lighting in your room is dim or if the group is large, even red can be difficult to see. When you aren't using your felt marker, cap it or it will dry out. When markers start squeaking, they are nearing retirement. Have pity on your learners; faint markers can be hard to read.

You may be wondering about markers. My favorite brand is "Mr. Sketch." They come in a variety of colors, are scented, nontoxic, and washable, and don't bleed through from one page to another. Note that there is a difference between felt markers for flip charts and dry markers, which are used on whiteboards.

Your lettering should be approximately 4 inches in height. Printing is easier to read than longhand. Upper and lower case is easier to read than all caps. Write telegraphically; use key words or phrases instead of full sentences.

Many trainers follow the 6 × 6 rule. This means no more than six words per line and no more than six lines per page. Remember to leave a couple of blank lines at the bottom because this area cannot always be seen by those sitting in the back of the room.

Before your group arrives, walk around the entire room so you can see what the group will see. Sit down in a chair and look at the flip chart to see how it will look through the occupant's eyes. A thorough preprogram check is important with any kind of visual aid. Unfortunately, people will often fail to alert you that they cannot see until the end of the program. Then they come up and tell you personally or put it on the evaluation. I hope these tips will keep you (and your participants in the back of the room) from flipping out!

Leslie

Dear Flipped Out:

*Pay attention to the markers you buy. Some of them **stink** and when used in a small, closed room can prove highly toxic! One more quick tip: As you use a flip chart, get in the habit of holding your markers upside down. When you hold them with the point up, all the ink runs to the bottom of the pen and when you start to write it will appear that the marker is running out of ink. Like so many of the Instant Trainer hints, this is a little thing, but it will help your learners (they'll be able to see what you're writing) and it will make you look like a pro.*

Chris

Dear Instant Trainers:

When my manager made me the new human resource specialist for our municipal employees, I was given a new flip chart as a "gift." Please don't get me wrong; it was a nice enough thing to do and I appreciate the gesture, but I'd rather have something more up to date. I mean, didn't flip charts go out with leisure suits and blue eye shadow? Will people in my diversity training sessions think I'm a fossil with my outdated piece of equipment? Please tell me your opinion about flip charts and any techniques you think I should know about, should I choose to use mine.

Skeptical in Saskatchewan

Dear Skeptical:

It may seem a bit behind the times, but an attractive, colorful flip chart can augment your presentation and save class time because you can have your material already written on it rather than doing so on the spot. Several little-known advantages of using a flip chart are that it provides you with "notes," keeps participants focused on major points, augments your lecture, and offers visual variety, even if it isn't very fancy.

You'll benefit from practicing with it a couple of times before you get in front of people so you can easily write on it, turn pages with ease, or tear them off neatly. I hope you'll work with the flip chart at least a couple of times so you can evaluate how it works for you.

Here are a few other tips. Most participants will dutifully write down anything you write on the flip chart, so reserve it for important points. If you have a complicated chart or diagram, give people a few minutes to copy it down before you begin explaining it because it's hard for participants to listen and write down a complicated piece of information. When you finish writing, wait for your learners to finish writing before you move on. Use this extra time to relax or to get yourself organized. Unless you have a specific reason not to do so, when you have finished with a particular page, flip it over so participants keep their attention focused on you.

A fun flip chart technique is the **revelation** method. If you have a prepared flip chart and have several items listed on a page, but want participants to see only one item at a time, you can cut strips of chart paper large enough to completely cover each printed item (one strip for each word or phrase). Then lightly tack the strip of paper at the top corners and top middle with small pieces of masking tape. Use only enough tape to hold the strip firmly in place. Follow this procedure with the entire page so that it appears blank from where the participants are seated. Then during your presentation you can remove one strip at a time whenever you wish to expose the information underneath. To ensure that each strip will be easily removed, one at a time, without interfering with any of the other strips, start at the bottom of the sheet rather than the top when covering them up.

Avoid talking to the group while you are facing the flip chart. Face the group, make your point, then turn and write. If you are quoting a phrase or making a statement, write down exactly what you say so people can begin writing when you begin speaking without having to change their notes. Once you've written the phrase and people have had a chance to write it down, then you can elaborate upon the idea.

There is also a high-tech flip chart / writing board with a plastic surface rather than individual sheets that you write on with a special pen. With the push of a button, you preserve your old information while exposing a clean writing surface. It will also make an 8 1/2 × 11 copy of what you wrote on the board. So, you don't have to be flipped out over the issue of using a flip chart; you could even blend the old with the new!

Leslie

Dear Skeptical:

I have to admit, I'm not as fond of flip charts as Leslie is, but there is one time when I'm always looking for my markers and a flip chart—when a group is brainstorming. When I want the group up and active, I always request multiple flip charts and plenty of new markers and figure out ways to get people into small working groups. I'm jazzed when I wander into a training room where the walls are covered with flip chart pages with lots of colors and lots of different handwriting. I'm always certain that this has been a session in which people were involved in the learning process.

 Chris

 Dear Instant Trainers:

I work for a state licensing and regulation agency and have been volunteered to offer a series of regulation updates for a large drugstore chain in our state. I'm not a complete stranger to public speaking, having worked in an ombudsman's office at a state university years ago, but I've been told to approach this more like a training than a briefing session. My boss has given me a series of overheads she had prepared when it was thought she would be the lucky person conducting these sessions. My question is about overhead projectors and the like. I mean, that's pretty old technology, isn't it? I remember overheads from when I was a kid. Am I going to date myself, my material, and my agency by depending on an overhead projector as my primary audiovisual tool?

Embarrassed in East St. Louis

Dear Embarrassed:

Actually, there's no need to feel dejected about the prospect of using an overhead projector. Even though, as you say, it's not the latest technology, today's trainers are still using them successfully. You didn't state whether you had your own equipment, but you have a couple of choices. If you'll be traveling throughout the state you might want to purchase one of the more compact projectors. 3M sells a briefcase model that works with a mirror (rather than a light projection process). It is portable, lightweight, and small, thus convenient for travel, but I find it a bit cumbersome to set up. I also use an Instaframe (more about that later) and it's impossible to use with the briefcase mirror model because it creates a double image.

Elmo, 3M, and Dukane all sell semiportable light projection models that are relatively convenient to cart around, and offer high lumens (high light density) and close focus. In my opinion, the brightness and quality of projection make up for the slightly larger size of the unit itself. So you see, Embarrassed, even though the overhead isn't quite like a high-tech slide show or computer projection, the manufacturers of these products have kept up with the times. You don't have to be embarrassed about using an overhead for your presentations; in fact, you can still create some pretty fancy transparencies and dazzle those drugstore employees. Now that we've filled you in on the overhead issues, please read the next question to find out more about producing quality transparencies!

Leslie

Dear Embarrassed:

I admit it, I'm an overhead junkie! I love their low-tech dependability and the ability to use them in most situations without turning off the lights. With that said, here's my best overhead tip. If you're not going to be using your own over-head (which you will, of course, keep very clean) you will encounter overheads that haven't been cleaned since the Eisenhower administration. I carry a small plastic spray bottle filled with glass cleaner and clean all the glass surfaces before a program. No, I'm not a cleaning freak (you should see my house), I've just seen what a smudge projected on an eight-foot screen looks like!

Chris

Dear Instant Trainers:

I read what you had to say about using overheads, and now I can't wait to hear your ideas on producing transparencies. I now know that there's more than one kind of overhead projector; does that mean there is more than one kind of transparency? Is there any kind of special equipment I need to produce overheads? What if I have no equipment of my own; can transparency production be outsourced? What if I have a limited budget? Have I asked too many questions?

Querulous in Quantico

Dear Querulous:

Just as overhead projectors vary, so do transparencies. Let's start with the most inexpensive option and move up. If you have a fairly recent model office copier, you can probably produce overhead transparencies right in your office. 3M produces several types of transparency stock, suitable for most copiers. Of course, this means you'll be working with black print, but we said we'd begin with basics, didn't we?

Transparency stock does come in colors, so even if you're restricted to black ink you could introduce some color into your presentation by using color transparencies (blue, yellow, and red are standard). There is also transparency stock designed to work with laser printers, so that's another option. If your budget is limited, these are your two best options.

Moving up on the scale is your color ink-jet printer. They can produce some pretty fancy transparencies and would add a touch of pizzazz to your training. One caveat: Keep your finished ink-jet process transparencies away from liquids. The color never fully penetrates the transparency and one spill means your image is washed away for good.

A more expensive option, should a windfall come your way, would be the heat transfer process. The colors are vivid and this is a perfect process for overhead transparency production. But it's more costly, too. Technology continues to make special features more affordable so I'd browse a few computer catalogs if I were you. Be aware that while transparencies produced through this process won't wash off, they can scratch, so you'll want to be careful with them.

Yes, you can outsource transparency production. It's expensive if the service bureau has to do everything from scratch, but if you have a computer you can create the overheads with a desktop publishing program or presentation software package. Then take your disk to a service bureau (such as Kinko's) for output. Classy color overhead transparencies add a nice dimension to your programs.

Leslie

Dear Querulous:

If you have Power Point and a modem you have access to a company called Genigraphics (see Appendix C). You can send them your overheads (or slides) electronically and they will print and return them in record time. Their support people are great to work with, they have unlimited patience in answering questions, and their prices are reasonable. Give them a call for a full description of their services.

One other hint: Any place with a color copier can make a color overhead. If you have a favorite photograph, a copy center can enlarge it and make it into a spectacular overhead. At least, it will be as spectacular as your picture was.

Make note of the word "enlarge." The rule of thumb is this: Make a paper copy of a potential overhead, drop it on the floor, and if you can read or see it well while standing up straight, an audience will be able to see it projected on a proper size screen. If you find yourself bending down to read it, you need to enlarge your text. If you must err either way, go larger, not smaller.

Chris

Dear Instant Trainers:

I am the Special Programs Coordinator for a state association of associations and I'm going to be offering a series of meetings for our members. In the past, I have introduced numerous speakers, welcomed attendees at state meetings, and officiated at panels, so I'm okay with the speaking part. Because of my position, though, I want to make sure I present a polished, professional training session. I plan to use overheads and am happy to report I have access to a color printer. What do I need to know about creating color transparencies: Are there any do's and don'ts or things I absolutely want to know? I'm eager to read your answer and get started!

Colorful in Crested Butte

Dear Colorful:

Assuming you have some sense of balance and design, you can have a great time creating color transparencies, and yes, there are a few things you want to keep in mind. The biggest mistake most people make initially is underutilizing the capacity of a color printer. Here's what I mean: They produce the letters or images in color, but don't do anything with the background. So they end up with a clear transparency with colored words or images. My question is, why would you do this? My philosophy is, if you have color, **use it!**

Saturate the transparency: Color the background. Use vivid colors, and use contrasting colors for effect. If you have a dark background, use light (yellow or white) colors for lettering, or vice versa. Avoid putting letters in colors that are the same relative value of your background because they'll be hard to read.

If you have a presentation software package such as Power Point or Astound, whether creating overheads or orchestrating a computer-driven presentation, be aware that the template you use may also be used by someone else at the same meeting. So do something to make your overheads different. You can import clip art from CDs or disks (see Appendix C) rather than restricting yourself to your presentation software package. This will give your overheads a special look.

Regardless of the printer you use for transparency production, take good care of your creations. They are expensive to produce and deserve a long, useful life. Now you're ready to venture out on your own: Just splash that color out there, make sure your letters are large enough (24 point and up), and remember to use enough contrast so your words stand out from the background. These simple principles will make your visuals easy for your members to remember!

Leslie

Dear Colorful:

One quick addition to Leslie's comments. When you frame your overheads (You do frame your overheads, don't you? Framed overheads are one way you can tell an amateur from a professional!) you have three choices. Here are my comments on each.

- *Cardboard Frames*
  These frames, available from any office supply store, allow you to tape your transparencies in a frame that will protect them and block out the light from around the edges. I use masking tape along all four sides to securely attach the transparency to the frame. You can use cardboard frames over and over. The drawback to these cardboard frames is that they add bulk and weight to your overheads, so if you travel with your overheads they may not be what you'll choose.

- *Plastic Sleeves*
  Companies like 3M make protective, plastic sleeves (3M calls them Flip Frames) that allow you to slide in your transparency, then fold out the edges and place them on the overhead. Usually they are three-hole punched on one side so you can keep your overheads in a binder for travel and storage ease. One caution: There seems to be a reaction between the color on a transparency and the plastic of the sleeve that destroys the overhead. I ruined a few color overheads before I figured this out. Another caution is that some frames aren't engineered to cover the three holes when the overhead is being projected. Those three holes don't look professional.

- *The Instaframe*
  The Instaframe is a plastic frame with edges and a glass panel that sits on the overhead bed. You simply put your unframed overhead in it and it projects like a framed overhead. This gadget eliminates the need for framing, making travel easier, keeps the overhead in place on the screen, and always looks professional. You can get your very own Instaframe from Creative Learning Tools or Creative Training Techniques. Both addresses are in Appendix C. Leslie and I carry our Instaframes everywhere we go. We've even been known to loan them to an unframed presenter!

Chris

PUTTING FUN IN YOUR TRAINING

Do you have to have fun during a training session?
No, only if you want somebody to learn something.

There is a growing body of research that confirms this offhand reply to a serious question. People learn and retain information better when they enjoy themselves. Perhaps it has to do with the *Third Grade Syndrome.*

Remember kindergarten? A worshipped teacher, recess, cookies, and milk. A great life! First and second grade were not all that different. Learning to read expanded your world, having your own scissors gave you a feeling of power, and you still got recess. Every day felt more like fun, not like learning. But think about the sheer volume of what you learned: the entire alphabet, upper and lower case, writing and reading, phonics, counting, adding, subtracting, and learning how to get along with the other children. Most of us, in those first three years of school, took in enormous amounts of information, retained it, and put it to use without even considering that we were studying and learning.

Then it happened. In the first or second week of September a slightly less forgiving teacher said, "Class, please remember, you're in the third grade now!" And you knew exactly what this meant. Long division, homework, and days without recess. You were becoming a grown-up. Life was becoming serious.

Most adults carry the memory of third grade into the training room. When they walk into your session they're wondering, "If I sit in the back row, can I avoid being called on? Can I stay awake during what is certain to be a boring few hours or, heaven help me, days? Will there be pop quizzes? Will I be embarrassed by something I say or do?"

Perhaps you're thinking, "This isn't school. I'm not a teacher." This is true, but now we're talking about trainees' feelings. Chances are they view anything that feels like education through a third-grade lens. Your job is to convince them that they're going to a pre-third-grade classroom instead. That's where the fun comes in.

Dear Instant Trainers:

Can a person be humor impaired? I can't tell a joke because I can never remember the punch line. People tell me you're supposed to make training sessions fun, but I seem to lack the ability to do it. What can I do?

Humorless in Houston

Dear Humorless:

Whoa, who said that the only way to have fun in a training session is for the trainer to be a stand-up comic? Telling jokes is probably the least preferred way to inject some fun into your training. Humor in a training session works best when it is the natural outgrowth of your participants' experiences and your subject's quirks.

There is a danger, however, with real-life humor. It should never be pointed at anyone. Humor in the classroom should always pull everyone closer together. It should never isolate an individual or group. That's why work and life experiences with a funny element are an experienced trainer's stock in trade.

You don't have to be solely responsible for bringing humor into your training sessions. Let's imagine you're conducting customer service training.

During your session, set aside some time, early on, to ask your participants to complete one of these sentences: "The funniest interaction I ever had with a customer was …" or, "The funniest thing that ever happened to me when I was a customer was…." Ask them to share their stories in small groups. Pay attention to the rise in energy level as they tell their tales. Ask each group to choose and tell the funniest story. After the stories are told you go to work, leading the debriefing. You'll be amazed how many of the points you were planning to make about customer service came out in between the laughs. (Bonus: Think of all the humorous stories you've just collected, and not a punch line among them!)

Here are a few simple rules to remember when using humor in training.

- Never use humor just for the sake of humor; always use humor that is relevant to the subject.
- It's better to practice your humor on a few people before you try it out in a session.
- Of course, off-color, racial, sexist, and ethnic humor are inappropriate and have no place in the training room.

Still looking for humor ideas? Try these:

- Start building a humor library. Start with *Making Humor Work* by Terry Paulsen, Ph.D., published by Crisp Publications.
- Think like a child. How can you make learning your subject feel like play? What's a silly way to remember the key points of your session?
- Read the *Reader's Digest* sections, Humor in Uniform, Life in These United States, etc. and look for a magazine called *Bonkers.*
- Read the rest of this chapter.

Think about humor as an opportunity to turn some ha-ha's into a-ha's!

Chris

Dear Humorless:

Expecting that because you're a trainer you have to be funny is like asking a participant to stand up and sing—it really puts the pressure on and may conflict with your self-perception. I agree with Chris that your life as a trainer will be more fun if you share the responsibility for humor with your learners. By collecting their humorous stories, funny remarks, and sponta-

neous reactions to unexpected events, you'll build your own humor reper-toire in no time!

Part of being funny is knowing what to look for. Once you start seeking humor out, you'll find obvious chuckles in the most surprising places: street signs and building directories, menus and product instructions (For example: Does orange juice really know how to concentrate? Do toothpaste and sham-poo really need directions?). If you see a humorous mistake or brief oddball article in your local newspaper, save it and read it to your group. People always appreciate a good laugh.

Using humor may feel like one more heavy responsibility initially, but watch how it lightens the atmosphere as nothing else can.

Leslie

Dear Instant Trainers:

I want to add an element of playfulness to my sessions and don't know where to start. Truth be told, I'm a keep-your-suit-jacket-on kind of trainer and I guess my discomfort gets in the way of my creativity. Most of the ideas I've come up with strike me as far too silly or cutesy for the work-place. Can you help me?

Stuffy in San Antonio

Dear Stuffy:

Have you seen those Word-a-Day calenders? If you had one, today's word would be PROPS. One of the easiest ways to add a bit of playfulness to your training session is to collect a trunkful of interesting, unusual, and creative things you can pull out and use during your training sessions. Maybe looking into my trunk will give you a better idea of what I mean.

- Packets of four Crayola crayons that I give participants to use dur-ing a creativity session.
- A weird-looking device called a space phone that consists of two large plastic cones connected by what looks like a very long slinky. Two people can talk to each other across a room but the sound is distorted. (Remember the old orange juice cans and strings?) I use these for both communication skills and telephone skills training.

- A large inflatable lightbulb that gets passed from one participant to another to reward the person who has expressed a good idea.

- Yellow plastic tape that says: Caution: Construction Zone. I use it to block off areas when the room is too large for the group.

One of the best ways to find props is to wander the aisles of the toy department of your favorite discount store. Make it a habit to peek into upscale toy stores every once in a while. Check the yellow pages to see if there is a teacher's supply store in your area. In mine, I found a nifty clock face you can project on your overhead to indicate when the session begins or when the break will be over.

You'll soon discover that training props come in two varieties. The first are items that relate to your topic. They can be children's versions of work-place staples. Consider a Fisher Price Tool Kit with each tool labeled to represent the skills you need to be an effective leader, a punching bag for conflict training, or even a button printed with your key message in a clever way.

The second variety are props you can use no matter what the topic: Noisemakers to bring a group back from a break or signal the end of an activity; Koosh balls to toss from trainee to trainee to solicit opinions during discussions; bags of very small toys (cars or animals, for example) that can be used to divide the group into teams; overhead pointers made in the shape of a hand with a finger pointing.

Here are a few simple rules to remember when you're using props:

- Props will be viewed as silly if they aren't linked tightly to your subject or don't serve a practical purpose in your session.

- Practice with your props before you use them in a session. You need to feel and look comfortable with them.

- Be sure the participants get to play with some of the props. It's not fair if you're the only one having all the fun!

Give props a try. If you end up with one that doesn't work, you're certain to know a kid who will thank you for it!

Chris

Dear Stuffy:

Maybe the words "keep-your-suit-jacket-on" were a tipoff to me, but I'm thinking you may not be ready to run out and buy a lifetime supply of

Koosh balls. Just in case I've correctly nailed your nature as "not into noise-makers," here are some alternatives that might help you venture out into the playful world of props.

You see, Stuffy, props can also include funny greeting cards you read to your group or buttons and stickers you give as rewards. You can simply hold up a funny T-shirt and hats with weird messages or other items that prompt a chuckle. The use of colorful, funny posters could jazz up your training room. Give people pieces of candy when they participate.

If you are at all uneasy about this issue, using cartoons can be a perfect way to begin stretching your comfort zone. Put some brain teasers on an overhead and ask your participants to solve them. Humorous quotations, attractively arranged on colored paper, overheads, or slides can offer comic relief.

For you Stuffy, perhaps the word of of the day is "caution." I suggest you start out small and slowly progress in your use of props so you give your funny bone a chance to grow.

Leslie

Dear Instant Trainers:

Last month I attended a wonderful training session where the presenter used a lot of humor, and it was a great experience. In a few weeks I will be conducting a series of training sessions for our management staff on selection interviewing as our company prepares for an expansion (I used to work as an employment recruiter). You can imagine I am paying close attention to how others teach. Although I'm certainly no stand-up comic, I have a good sense of humor and have experienced a few oddball "adventures in interviewing" that I think could make great examples. My question is this: Does one use humor just for humor's sake or is there some kind of strategy behind using humor in a training program?

Comedic in Kauai

Dear Comedic:

In a word, yes! Humor can simply be used for its own sake. Giving people a chance to laugh while covering a serious topic offers a welcome break for your learners. Humor helps people relax, helps you make a point, and provides physical and emotional relief during a long training session. The energizing effects of humor are undeniable. But there's another strategy for using humor, too. I am of the opinion that strategically positioned humor can boost learning and retention. The next time you have the opportunity to observe a skilled trainer or speaker, you might notice him or her using humor as a prelude to learning points. Let me explain.

Laughter affects us mentally and physically. Blood pressure momentarily drops, tension is released, and inhibitions are lessened. And there's more: When we laugh, we suspend judgment. When we suspend judgment we lose many of our defenses; our minds open to possibilities.

I like to take advantage of this state in my training sessions. I intentionally tell a humorous story or relate a funny experience, employing odd body language or facial expressions, and while people are still laughing, I interject a serious point. Now, I may still have a smile on my face when I say it, and people may still feel tickled by the humorous part of what I said, but the "laughtermath" (as I like to call it) is the perfect time to interject a memorable point. I perceive this as perfect timing because people's minds are still disarmed from the humor. People's defense mechanisms are down, which means they're in a state of increased receptivity. Although I have no research to back it up, I am of the opinion that people are more inclined to remember ideas and stories that are linked with a laugh or smile. And maybe they're more likely to seriously consider something when it is packaged with a smile. You might look for this in a presenter, and try it yourself. Comic relief is a great momentary energizer, but it can also be used as an effective vehicle for delivering your most serious material.

Leslie

Dear Comedic:

I couldn't agree more, with one big exception: joke telling. Back in the dark ages, people were taught that you needed to start a training session with a joke. So they went to the 1001 Jokes to Get Them Laughing *book, chose one that made them laugh, and put it into their presentation.*

People want and need to laugh more on a daily basis, but in a training session there needs to be some connection between the humorous story or exercise and the subject of the class. Your past experiences as a recruiter are perfect. If you had a series of resume or interview question bloopers, you could sprinkle them throughout your session as rewards for returning from breaks on time, to transition from one part of your material to another, or as energizers when you sense the group tiring. Learning to use relevant humor is a valuable training skill!

Chris

Dear Instant Trainers:

Yesterday I was looking through a trainer's catalog and noticed a book called *Games Trainers Play*. I didn't know trainers were playing games. I'm alone in my training department, so how could I get on a team? What's the point of trainers playing games?

Solo in SoHo

Dear Solo:

The games that skillful trainers play aren't with other trainers, they're with their trainees. If you had the opportunity to explore any of the four books in Ed Scannell and John Newstrom's excellent series, *Games Trainers Play,* (available from McGraw-Hill; 1-800-2 MCGRAW), you would have learned that games in training are a special subset of group activities that work well to liven up a training session while enhancing learning.

Here's what Ed and John think makes a game. They:

- are brief
- are participative
- are low risk
- are single-focus

- are inexpensive
- use props
- are adaptable

I would add one thing to their list: Games are fun!

Games can be modeled after TV productions: a Customer Service Family Feud and New Employee Orientation Jeopardy, for example. The children's classics, 20 Questions as a review or Simon Says for learning a process, and some traditional favorites, Trivial Pursuit based on an organization's history, are all good possibilities.

Games can be used for icebreakers. As people enter the room, give them a slip of paper with a character's name (Sonny for example). Instruct them to find their partner in the group. Sonny would, of course, be looking for Cher. If you have an odd number of participants, add Huey, Dewey, and Louie to the mix.

Games can be used as reviews. There are simple software packages that allow you to make crossword puzzles for which you can choose the words. Create one that has the key concepts of your session, divide the group into teams and see who completes the puzzle first.

Games can be used as energizers. Consider a scavenger hunt in the middle of the afternoon. If you were doing communication training in an urban area, you could send trainees out in teams to find examples of signs that communicate well or miss the mark. During a technical training session, you could order the makings for ice cream sundaes and have a contest to see who makes the most artful or tasty creation.

Here are a few simple rules to remember when using games.

- Any game needs to make sense in the context of your session. Trainees will resent playing that doesn't connect with the learning.

- Practice! Don't try a game for the first time in front of a group. Work out all the kinks before the real thing. (You might want to read our response to Directionless in Detroit in Chapter 13 about giving instructions as a part of your preparation.)

- As you start planning your game, avoid complexity. Like many things in life, simple is better.

When you develop a good game you can send it in to Ed Scannell and John Newstrom. Maybe it will be selected for their next book!

Chris

Dear Solo:

If you're still stuck at the starting line with the games issue, purchase one of the renowned Games Trainers Play *series books and work your way up from there. Start with the simplest, quickest games until you feel more confident. In no time at all you'll be calling the signals for bigger and better learning games. Appendix D lists additional titles that will help you and your trainees have more fun in your sessions.*

All games don't have to be organized events. They can simply be fun or spontaneous moments. For example, if you teach computer training, before your session begins, you could place small colored stickers on the bottoms of a few of the keyboards (think of how door prizes are given out at a conference) and periodically give away a piece of candy or another small token to the person with a particular color sticker.

Games can be as simple as a sentence-completion project: Get participants into small groups and ask them to complete a sentence destined to be funny, such as, "You know it's going to be a bad day at work when...."

If you know any experienced trainers, ask them for their favorite games and pretty soon you'll have a great collection to play with.

Leslie

DEALING WITH DIFFICULT TRAINEES

*Keep the chips off your shoulder and in your hand so you
have control over where they fall.*

If you've ever watched a skilled athlete perform, you have witnessed a triumph of mind over matter: hard work that appears effortless in the execution. In any venue, performing at your best requires a delicate balance of control and letting go, a way of staying focused while learning to get out of your own way. Eastern philosophy is rich with stories about the continuing conflict between simultaneously maintaining control and letting go.

As a trainer, you will be asked to consistently perform at your best, sometimes under the worst of circumstances. Some of your learners will bring their history of negative classroom experiences with them. You'll witness fear, insecurity, defensiveness, and resistance. Sometimes you'll need to control the behaviors attached to these attitudes and sometimes you'll need to let go.

As you read this chapter, consider the many ways you can defuse, deflect, and redirect people's negative energies. You won't always know why people are resistant or combative, but your job is to get your message across in spite of it all. Stay neutral and objective. When part of you wants to take control or force an issue, stop and investigate your intent. Are you trying to teach a lesson or learn a lesson?

This will help you handle upset or difficult people more effectively. You can't control what others do, but you can control what you do. This chapter highlights numerous strategies, tools, and techniques for helping people break through their barriers so they can hear what you have to say. Perhaps it's no surprise that the less you worry about maintaining control the more control you'll actually have. The trainers who know how to handle difficult people are masters at letting go—they have already dealt with their own issues. Just like other skilled performers, they make the process of exercising control look deceptively easy by skillfully getting out of the way.

Dear Instant Trainers:

Yesterday I did my first training session and I was so afraid no one would participate but the opposite happened. I had one guy who I couldn't shut up. He acted as if he was the only one in the room, and it seemed that he had a question or comment for everything I said. I wanted participation, but this was too much. How can I handle this next time?

Nonplussed in Nantucket

Dear Nonplussed:

What a perfect example of too much of a good thing! Even audience participation isn't always good, when it's only one audience member who is participating. I still remember an evaluation comment from 20 years ago that read, "I wish someone had stuffed a sock in Cliff's mouth!" Here, in escalating order, are strategies for pacifying the over-participator.

First, ignore the raised hand (even if it comes with the "flip" on it that begs for attention) and respond to other trainees who have their hands up.

Now, maybe you're thinking, "What if no one else has raised a hand?" Stay with me. If no one else raises a hand, make your questions easier to answer, or give your group a chance to warm up to the topic by priming the pump. Let them briefly discuss the issue among themselves (pairs are quick) and then ask what they covered. I love to ask "What did your partner have to say?" because people are often more inclined to report what someone else said rather than to self-report.

Now back to our over-participators. Maybe ignoring the raised hand doesn't work. As other participants are raising their hands, look the overzealous trainee in the eye and say, "I'm not ignoring you …" (but you are). Then add, "I'd like to get a couple of other comments first." This acknowledges that there are others present in the room and your expectation is that everyone will participate. After you've garnered a few other comments, go back to the person you put off for a few minutes.

If all else fails, try to speak with the person one on one during break or lunch time. Approach him or her privately and say, "I appreciate your participation, **and** (it is important that you use the word "and" rather than "but") I would love to get a few others to participate, too. So if you raise your hand and I don't respond, it's simply because I'm trying to get others involved. I hope you don't mind. If you like, make a note of any questions I don't answer and I'd be happy to do so after our program."

If this individual is constantly referring to his or her situation and you've begun to see rolling eyes and looks of resignation, it's time to up the ante. Here's a way of respecting your participant while setting limits: Say something like, "I'm getting the sense that your situation is unique and quite unlike what others in this room are experiencing. So that I can meet the needs of everyone here, I'd like to keep our discussion focused in a more general sense. But I'd like to talk with you, one on one, immediately after the program."

If the person is simply a showboater, he or she will usually clam up (and also be the first to leave). If there is truly a need, the person will happily stay after the program to talk with you. From the group's perspective, you have saved them from searching for a sock. You have also exhibited respect for an individual while recognizing the needs of your group. You've been kind and generous. And you've maintained control in a most tactful and subtle way. These tactics and strategies might help you feel less challenged and more in charge.

Leslie

Dear Nonplussed:

This is a one of a trainer's worst nightmares. It's hard not to feel uncomfortable as you go through Leslie's suggestions. Please keep in mind that you need to control the program, so that all the learners have the opportunity to get what they need out of the session. Just as you'd feel an obligation to encourage a nonparticipator, you have an obligation to stop one person from dominating the conversation. Trust me, your learners will appreciate your efforts to make sure everyone is involved!

Chris

Dear Instant Trainers:

I have good news and bad news. The good news is that as the new corporate wellness coordinator, I get to teach a series of four "For the Health of It" programs for all our staff. I've always wanted to do this kind of thing so I am excited to finally reach my goal. But so far, I seem to be standing alone in the enthusiasm camp! Frankly, I'm shocked and appalled at the lack of enthusiasm on the part of our employees. The bad news: This will be mandatory training. Everyone will go through my wellness program at some point. I feel so strongly about my topic and the benefits staff will receive that I think I can handle some initial resistance, but I am wondering if there is anything special I can do to help put people at ease despite their obligatory presence. Any ideas?

Enthused in Eau Claire

Dear Enthused:

Indeed, some participants resist being "sent" to any kind of program, especially one that requires significant behavior change, so you have two initial strikes against you. I would like to compliment you on your attitude though, because that is one big hurdle you won't have to contend with. Here is a strategy that worked well with hundreds, perhaps thousands, of "captive state employee trainees." It's based on the principle that "There is no bad news." Because of your positive attitude, you're halfway there already. You sense that if there's an issue looming in the midst of your audience, you need to acknowledge it, bring it out in the open before people will listen to you, and find a way to lay it aside before you can get down to work.

Here's the strategy: Recognize people's obliged presence as a standard part of your getting-acquainted routine. If you didn't know better, you could ask, "How were you selected for this program?" which would elicit some truthful (or resentful comments), but you already know that. We only included that question for those readers who may have a mixture of mandated and elected participants. Now, let's go to the next steps.

1. Openly acknowledge the conditions under which participants are attending.

    Do not apologize, but acknowledge by saying something like, "As you know, our company has elected to conduct this wellness program for all of our staff. While the ideal might be that you'd all voluntarily sign up for this training, we want to ensure that everyone has the opportunity to learn about wellness and what it means to you...."

2. Adjust their perspective.

    "You can think of time you're spending in these classes and the content of this program series as an investment—in yourself. Even if you left the company tomorrow, all of the information you learn in this series will belong to you and you alone...."

3. Make a statement of your commitment.

    "You have my commitment that I'll take every measure to make this wellness series a worthwhile experience for you...."

4. Then, ask for their commitment.

    "Maybe you wouldn't choose to be here—but you are here, and you are going to learn some surprisingly practical tips and strategies you can immediately apply in your life. I hope you're ready to take advantage of this new information."

Avoid apologizing, preaching, or making a big issue of it. You already anticipate some initial resistance, and if you maintain that positive attitude of yours, you will succeed in turning the situation around. You are astute to realize that touchy issues such as mandatory attendance must be acknowledged and tactfully laid aside because if they aren't, they will needlessly block the learning process.

Leslie

Dear Enthused:

We're both great believers in stating the obvious. If you don't do it up front, you can lose lots of valuable training time. Since you're going to be doing this program over a period of time, pay close attention to the comments of those who attend the first few sessions. If you can capture any of their statements or stories, ones that tell how they realized the value of the wellness programs, use them in later sessions. I did mandatory diversity training for a utilities firm and during the third session one of the workers told us about the difficulties his daughter had in the Navy. I asked his permission to share his story in other classes and it became a powerful tool I used to help other people realize that diversity may not be something that's important to them, but is something that affects us all. Good luck!

Chris

Dear Instant Trainers:

I am now the lucky individual who gets to conduct new employee orientations. Now, don't get me wrong, I like the company I work for, but frankly, what could be more boring than four hours of facts, faces, and fluff about our organization that people will never remember? I remember what a yawn it was when I went through my orientation a few years ago, and (how can I say this?) while our company has grown and expanded, I'm not sure how much I could include about the process that would generate excitement. I hate being bored, and I hate being boring, so I'm trying to figure out how I could add some pizzazz to a pretty dry topic. I love my job and I work for a great company, but we're sort of vanilla when it comes right down to it. Any ideas?

Bored in Barrow

Dear Bored:

Yes, employee orientations can be a challenge, and it's a good thing you're aware of the fact that you need to warm up your attitude about this topic before you can get anyone else to appreciate it. While a company or organization's history may seem like a yawn to you, a few new employees might find it interesting. First of all, could you give the orientation in two 2-hour blocks instead of one 4-hour session? A shorter time frame may be just what you're looking for.

Whether you offer your orientation in bite-size portions or one big gulp, here are a few things you could do to jazz things up.

Icebreaker:

If you have a small group of new employees, let them get acquainted with each other. There are many resources on icebreakers, and the best ones are relevant for attendees. Who are you, where did you last work, and what brought you to this company are a few good starter questions. As you already know, thorough orientations involve a handout or workbook for later reference, historical and market information, productivity markers, a description of products or services, vendors, annual figures, and information on structure, systems, benefits, and codes of conduct. Safety issues, confidentiality, departmental relationships, culture, and philosophy (vision, mission, value statements) are also nice.

Here are a few creative approaches to employee orientations:

- slide shows with music that humorously overstates its position (the theme from *Mission Impossible,* for example)

- presenting the different pieces of information as a board game

- offering facts and figures like parts of a Trivial Pursuit or Jeopardy game

- letting people participate by making a guessing game of historical information or current market status (using multiple choice answers)

- giving little prizes when using any kind of game format

- adding tidbits of insider information (this is the _____ department, otherwise known as…)

- creating bumper sticker slogans and humorous nicknames for different departments

- interjecting odd bits of historical information in between the factual, necessary items

- writing an in-house funny song or poem

- writing down the most common (or essential) questions and answers most new employees ask and all of them need to know, passing the completed cards out and letting each person read a card, which includes a central question plus the answer

- displaying examples of your products (if that's your business) and letting people take a good look at them

- creating a visual display: several panels of pictures, photos, or icons that create a pictorial history of your organization and walking people through each panel so they can connect the parts with the whole
- showing a series of cartoons that relate to your different topics as you present them

As you can see, Bored, you can get really creative with an employee orientation. My sense is that you just don't want to be a talking head, throwing out assorted bits of information without making any real connection with your participants. By letting them be a natural part of the process, and by making their time spent with you an enjoyable experience, you can change the face of your company's employee orientations for good. I hope this puts a big, warm smile on your face (as it will the faces of your participants)!

Leslie

Dear Bored:

After that long list of ideas, I'm sure you thought I wouldn't have any more. Of course I do; how about a tour? Most organizations have tours for civic groups or Girl Scout troops, but hardly ever take their own people on a tour. You could arrange a tour with stops at major areas. Invite a person from each department to spend a few minutes explaining want happens in this part of the organization. This applies to small organizations as well as large companies. Most people don't have a clear understanding of all the functions of their organization. Tours get people up and moving, help them learn their way around the building, and put faces to the names they've been hearing. I promise, you won't be bored!

Chris

 Dear Instant Trainers:

In addition to my regular duties, my boss just appointed me as the new Quality Coordinator. I'm actually rather excited about this, but one of my coworkers (who has had some experience in quality work) wanted this assignment. My boss thinks I have a better attitude and more rapport with our work team. As you can guess, my attitude is a bit mixed at the moment, since I think I'm going to have an uphill battle with this team member for a while (I'm already getting the cold shoulder and those awful sideways glances from this individual). I've seen this person get competitive and try to take over a meeting in the past. How can I defuse this person's jealousy and judgment in our Quality Meetings while somehow maintaining dignity (for both of us)?

Mutiny in Minot

Dear Mutiny:

How good of you to ask! Wouldn't the world be great if you could simply enjoy your new position without someone's bad attitude getting in the way! But here are some suggestions that will help:

1. Do everything you can to keep from getting emotionally hooked. This person may attempt to take the control away from you to prove who the real quality "expert" is. You can prevent this. Embrace the concept that "There is no bad news." This means that, regardless of what someone says or does in your meeting, you can neutralize the anger, hostility, resistance, or resentment by responding in a manner that reflects neutrality or acceptance of that person's idea. If, at any point, this person does make a worthy comment, say a simple "Thank you." Additional neutral responses involve saying things like, "I appreciate your comment," or "I see," or, "That might work with our team." The advantage of responding with positive or neutral statements such as these is that you have given the person nothing to push against. It will be hard for this individual to create too much of a disturbance if you reinforce good comments and politely refuse to push back when he or she tries to fight with you.

2. Redefine or deflect challenging comments without making them an issue. This is a subtle spin on the strategy we just covered. If the person says something practical or possible, you can use it as an example. This often serves two purposes: The person gets positive attention and recognition, and you achieve your purpose of staying on target. "I agree with your comment about _____; you're right. We could try that in our team ..." or "Earlier, _____ brought up an alternate approach to the process model we are proposing...." You can also redefine a statement as

a way of deflecting what the person just said: "If what you are saying is...." Then find the kernel of commonality between that person's statement and your position.

3. Do what you can to let the person save face. You do not need to "win" a battle with this person, nor do you have to raise the issue of who is wrong and who is right. Give the person some space. "My intention is to avoid a position of total right and total wrong; we don't need to agree on every issue. What we do need is to find a workable structure for our team so we can move forward in our quality efforts." If the person insists on pushing you or creating a stalemate, you can dismiss it by saying,"I have a different opinion ..." and hope you can drop it at that.

4. Recognize the person's expertise and ask for alternative suggestions or approaches. Your team member may have some excellent suggestions. If so, this is a chance for this individual to step into the limelight. Say, "Based on your experience with quality teams, I wonder if you might have some ideas on how we might want to approach this situation ..." or "I'm interested in your opinion." This kind of disarming approach is a peace offering of sorts: You recognize the person's expertise, you ask for an opinion, and the group witnesses this exchange. If you get a negative or petulant response, everyone gets a sense of where this person is coming from. If you get helpful, practical information, everyone benefits, including your conflicted colleague.

5. If the conflict or resistance reaches intolerable proportions, confront the person whose behavior is detrimental to the group before you get too intimidated or angry. There is an old training axiom: *Never throw away your group for the sake of one person.* Many work teams or training audiences have been turned off to learning by a conflict that existed between the trainer or facilitator and a recalcitrant participant. Try coming to terms by first speaking to the individual in private: "I'm hearing you make some statements about (me, our quality efforts) and I sense you have some strong opinions. I'd like to discuss this issue with you." If you get nowhere, at least you know you tried.

Trust your work team. If they see nothing but resistance and criticism from this individual while they witness your attempts to help, draw out, and include your colleague, the group will quickly figure out what's going on and you will have their support. They may simply tune out the individual or someone may take the initiative and speak out. By putting your own spin on these strategies you will come up with some ways to control your meetings without undue conflict. A little bit of tact and respect can go a long way in helping salve someone's needy ego.

Leslie

Dear Mutiny:

Hostile participants are no fun. The easiest route is to hope that they will go away. Usually they don't, so you'll have to deal with the situation. The key to this situation is preparation. If you take the time to think through your role in the interactions and practice beforehand the kinds of comments you want to make, you'll get better results. If you get to the point that you need to have a private conversation with the other person, here is a phrase I've found to be helpful: "When you ... (describe the behavior) ... then I ... (describe your reaction) ..." This simple statement does two things: It focuses on the behavior, not the person; and it causes you to own your reaction. It can be followed by, "In the future it would be more helpful for me if you would ... (describe the new behavior)." This pattern allows you to keep your discussion focused on actions rather than personalities. This is one of the toughest issues a trainer can face. Hang in there. You're learning some valuable lessons that apply to a lot more than just training!

Chris

 Dear Instant Trainers:

I certainly wish I had known about you last week; I could really have used your expertise! You see, I work for an accounting firm and in addition to our accounting services, last year we began offering a series of professional development programs for clients who request it. Now, there are some accountants who might not want to speak to more than three people at a time, but I enjoy it. I thoroughly enjoyed my first two sessions with one of our major clients, but last week I worked with a different department in their organization and it was like daylight and darkness. I worked with what had to be the toughest group in the world; they put new meaning to the word indifferent. I mean, it was like trying to teach stones how to move! Come to think of it, I think stones would have been easier.

In my first session, people responded. The second time I covered the same material with a different group, participation was great. The third time it was a disaster. I wanted to stop and check pulses every 15 minutes to make sure everyone was still breathing, only I wasn't teaching aerobics! What happened? I thought we had built trust, and were ready to work, but these folks had the worst collective case of apathy I have ever witnessed. Which brings me to my burning question: When faced with an apathetic, indifferent audience, are there any tips or techniques for breaking through?

Burning in Bradenton

Dear Burning:

You've experienced one of the most challenging situations a trainer can face, whether seasoned pro or brand new to the game. At least resentful or resistant people have some kind of observable behavior! Apathy and indifference give you little to go on. But here's something I've learned about human behavior that relates to your situation: People behave in ways that make sense to them. When you get a whole group that has lapsed into an apathetic response, there could be several reasons. For example, they may be trying to teach someone a lesson (probably not you; perhaps a supervisor or manager), but of course, you bear the brunt of their payback. Also, the group may not fully understand your role. Or they may understand it and not care.

Additionally, your program and why it is being held may have been misrepresented or explained poorly. People often resent being in a training session when there appears to be no need or relevancy. Their presence may have been mandated. Or they may have recently attended a similar session. You may or may not ever know the whys and wherefores. What you do know, though, is that when faced with indifference and apathy, you want to punch through it respectfully but firmly.

It's not as if you can pretend these behaviors don't exist, so I would recommend laying it on the line with your group and waiting to see what happens. The next time you face an unresponsive group, try this:

1. Acknowledge the situation using behavioral, objective language (rather than relying on interpretive or judgmental words). "I'm accustomed to having questions and comments at this point in the program and right now I'm not getting any...."

2. State your observations (what you see and hear rather than your interpretations).

"What I am observing is very little eye contact and some side discussions instead of comments directed to me or to the group. When I ask a question I'm not seeing any raised hands...."

3. Inquire and assist (this is the confrontation). You want to express sincere concern, objectivity, and an expectation that people will be straight with you.

"I'd like to find out what's going on with you right now so we can figure out what to do about it...."

4. Explore, commit, and adapt. Extend a spirit of service to your group. Explain your intent as directly as you can so they understand you are serious about this issue.

"It is my intention to offer you some essential (skills) (information) ...." People are often indifferent if they feel the material is irrelevant or beneath their skill level, or that they are being forced to take part in something that lacks meaning to them. Explain that you'll do your absolute best to meet their needs.

I have had great luck with this approach. It simply asks participants to take responsibility for their behavior. Usually, when people realize they've been "found out" and they can't get away with covert rebellion or emotional withdrawal, they come around. By the time we get to step 4, some brave soul has usually explained what is going on and a spirited discussion ensues. It's a cathartic experience, and a powerful one as you can imagine, and it's worked for me every time, with varying levels of success.

I hope this will work for you. If nothing else, you will have won people's respect because you refused to buy into their negative behaviors. By listening to their perceptions and feelings, you acknowledge them as human beings. That in itself is pretty powerful. While I wouldn't wish an apathetic group on you, I expect that the next time you're faced with apathy or indifference, people will warm up after your tactful confrontation rather than continue to feel burned up over what's bugging them.

Leslie

Dear Burning:

Did I remember you saying the people in your session were employees of one of your firm's major clients? That may put a different spin on your actions. Any time you're in the position of training people in someone else's organization (especially if it's a client's business) you may need to tread lightly. Under normal circumstances I would follow Leslie's advice to the letter, but if I were in your shoes and on a client's turf I'd take a slightly different approach.

After sensing the indifference I'd do a quick mental review of my program so far and make certain I'd spent enough time clearly tying my subject to the participants' world. If I hadn't, I'd do that immediately. If I felt I had, I'd call a break as soon as one would fit comfortably in the material and find the person who had invited me to do the presentation. This would be the person I'd use Leslie's formula on in a quick conversation.

Often there are issues within an organization that would be awkward for you, as a supplier, to get in the middle of. Your discussion with your contact may help you decide what you want to say to the participants. Either way, you'll be better prepared when you go back to the training room.

Chris

Dear Instant Trainers:

I've worked in the retail food industry for well over a decade and I love my work. We have two stores in a mid-size town and have recently converted to a new computerized cash register system. I can't believe how resistant people are to our new system. Despite the fact that inventory, pricing, and reorders will be handled by our new system, I'm getting all kinds of flack from our employees. We can't go back; the technology is here and it can help us as a company. I want my people to feel as excited as I am about this new system but so far all I'm getting are complaints and resistance. What they need to understand is that the learning process never stops, and once we adjust to our computers we start working on ourselves. Our next project is customer service and then teamwork. We need to get this resistance out of the way. How do you suggest I handle these attitudes?

Sacked in Saginaw

Dear Sacked:

First of all, let me hand it to you. Despite the resistant attitude of your employees you sound pretty upbeat, and this is essential. The many benefits of your new system aren't fully evident yet, and I'd guess that's one of the reasons you're getting resistance. People don't always like changing how they do things, and introducing new technology demands new ways of thinking and behaving. This is difficult. As you said, personal change will follow, and that will be difficult, too.

I have found that one effective way of breaking through resistance is to let people do it for themselves rather than letting the trainer doing it for them. Here's what I mean: If you try to explain logically why employees should embrace the new system, people will tune you out. But if you give *them* the chance to work things through, you may get an entirely different response.

What if you were to pose some substantive questions for a group of employees:

> "What are the disadvantages for you of our introducing a new system?"
>
> "What are the advantages?"
>
> "What's the toughest part about learning this new system?"
>
> "What might happen to us competitively if we don't move along with available technology?"

You might think of some additional questions, too. Letting people lead themselves through a series of good questions is a powerful process. Most of them know, deep in their hearts, that this change is necessary. They even know that they'll ultimately benefit, but they need an arena in which they can complain, express their concerns, and commiserate. Often, after they've been able to blow off steam and feel they've been listened to, they're ready to move on.

Once you get to the service and teamwork skills training, you can ask your participants to list their own advantages and disadvantages of the self-improvement process. I'm sure you've gotten the point. Teach in such a way that your learners can also learn from themselves and each other. The group synergy will help drive personal change, too. I hope once your employees are allowed to express their initial concerns about all the changes, they'll be willing to shelve their resistance for good!

Leslie

Dear Sacked:

Training doesn't solve everything. Far from it! We know that way too often people think training is a magic cure-all for everything that's less than perfect in an organization. In your case, the time you spend working to get people ready for the change your grocery store is facing is more important than the actual training on the new cash register system. Hard to believe a trainer would say this, but I would encourage you to think through this process carefully and worry about the training later!

Chris

Dear Instant Trainers:

I work for a regional power company and we've recently initiated quality teams. This is a new concept for us, and a brand new one for me. A local consultant suggested we begin by offering a series of trust- and team-building sessions which will be highly interactive. People will be asked to do a good deal of group work. I get to be the leader of these meetings and I'm relieved to say I don't have to develop the materials. We've purchased a series of team exercises and activities for this purpose. My job is to pull it all together with brief lecture bits on our vision and mission, and conduct the debriefings following our group activities.

As our goal is improved communication and cross training, people will be asked to get into different groups every time we run an activity. We will have about 20 people per session and I would like to know the most effective ways to get people to change from one group to another. I've found that participants "bond" quickly and don't like the idea of going from one set of teammates to another. What advice do you have for me?

Regrouping in Racine

Dear Regrouping:

You're right; people don't always like moving from one table (or one group) to another, but here are some thoughts. First of all, work on your expectation level. If you expect resistance you may well get it. So just assume that everyone will go along. One thing we've found to be consistently true is that, when it comes to getting people into groups, most of the time they would rather have you organize the process than ask them to make the decision. Next, think creatively and try to envision all the different ways you can get people into groups:

- You can number people off into groups (one by one, people call out a number, beginning with one, up to the number of groups you want).
- You can do the same with the alphabet.

- You can use color coding (colored dots or a series of them on each person's name badge) and shift them from one color or combination to the other.

- You can ask participants to draw an item out of a hat (straws of various lengths, shapes, numbers, animals, foods, etc.) and let each item designate a group.

What you do is probably less important than how you do it. Your positive expectations and dash of creativity can make a big difference as to whether you get groans or grins when you ask people to group up.

Leslie

Dear Regrouping:

People's reluctance to changing groups often comes from a fear of being left out. Remember how it felt when you were in the third grade and were the last one picked for a sports team? Many adults carry that discomfort inside. Your job is to make changing teams a risk-free process. As long as you give participants the assurance they won't be embarrassed and left out, they'll usually cooperate. Leslie's suggestions combined with all the imaginative things I know you'll come up with will give your trainees the safety net they need to feel comfortable as they do the training equivalent of "change partners and dance."

Chris

 Dear Instant Trainers:

As a new trainer, I've heard lots of horror stories about participants who won't shut up in a training session, but I've got two who won't open up. Now, maybe it's just me. I'm new to this field and have lots to learn, but I have two people in my interpersonal communication series who just don't participate. This may just be my insecurity speaking, but I'd feel a whole lot better if I could get everyone in my session to buy in. Any ideas on how to draw in the nonparticipative participant?

Clammed up in Chattanooga

Dear Clammed:

If it weren't for extremes we wouldn't have averages, now would we! I can appreciate your concern and here are some thoughts on drawing in the non-participator without putting undue pressure on the individual in question. As I am unsure whether this person is totally uninclined to participate or simply very quiet, I'll offer a variety of suggestions. You want to be subtle; the last thing you want to do is single the person out right off the bat. Conducting a one-on-one role play or discussion is usually an effective way to get everyone talking together.

If you pass out materials or handouts during your session, you could begin by handing the person a small stack of your materials, requesting that they be passed to everyone else at the table. A small gesture, but it's participation! If you hear this individual make a worthy statement anytime during a discussion, ask about it once the whole group is back in full session. Make sure it's a positive example so the person doesn't feel embarrassed.

Engage participants in a paired discussion and when you debrief, ask the person you most want to participate if he or she has any ideas, suggestions, or input following your activity. Try engaging the person in conversation during break time. Get to know this individual; find out something special about the person and remember it. Just think of this situation as trying to draw out a shy puppy or kitten. A positive attitude, a little bit of time, and your positive persistence will not only help you bring out another person's best, it will also help you bring out yours.

Leslie

Dear Clammed:

Sometimes the best way to approach shy animals is to ignore them. To apply this piece of advice in a training session is tricky and takes some careful observation on your part. There are some people in the world whose participation happens internally. The fact that they're not verbally active in a class doesn't mean they're not learning. To determine the difference between this person and a true non-participator takes practice. Here are a few clues to look for.

- *An introvert is likely to take notes; a true non-participator seldom does.*

- *An introvert is likely to participate in an activity, although not necessarily verbally; a true non-participator seldom joins in.*

- *An introvert is likely to talk in a small group discussion; a true non-participator seldom does.*

- *An introvert is likely to ask you a question during a break; a true non-participator seldom asks anything unless it has to do with when the session will be over.*

If you decide your non-participant is an introvert, respect his or her quiet, less outgoing approach to learning. If, on the other hand, you decide you are dealing with non-participators, you need to help them. Explain how getting involved will help them, the other learners, and you!

Chris

CAPITALIZING ON DIVERSITY

May we find words and ways to connect our
common threads.

A symphony or a fog horn: which would you rather listen to? A lively melody or the same single, unchanging note, repeating itself over and over again? While there may be some comfort in hearing the familiar bellow of a fog horn's repeated tone, with the passage of time, we are apt to cease hearing it at all. Just as lighthouses and fog horns have become things of the past, so has our homogeneous society. We are a cacophony of contrast in our cities and workplaces. We are diverse.

The trainer who can capitalize on the patchwork of backgrounds, outlooks, skills, and orientations enriches the learning experience for everyone. A turn of phrase, inclusive references, respectful speech, and a open mind reflect your desire and willingness to learn about others. As you, the trainer, set the stage, your audience will follow.

Sometimes we forget the multiple levels of teaching that happen in a session. It's not just the content we've prepared, or even how we present it. Our attitudes and perceptions set the tone. We are the models of our messages and the purveyors of our convictions. What our participants incidentally see and hear us do is often a more memorable lesson than our most profound lecture.

This chapter provides you with various ways of understanding and respecting diverse learners. Audience analysis teaches us to prepare our message in such a way that it will be heard. Working with diverse audiences is a part of the process and the more you develop your diversity skills, the fewer differences you will see. What someone looks like, how they live, or the special circumstances under which they live are immaterial. That they are there to learn is the point. The more we learn about each other, the more we will gravitate toward what we hold in common.

And just as the fog horn's solitary note disappears into the backdrop of other noise, the day will come when we will no longer discern the visual differences between ourselves. We will instead honor what we hold in common. We are all learners. We are all people. Let us learn.

 Dear Instant Trainers:

I'm really proud of our organization. In addition to producing quality products, delivered with exceptional service, we've been talking and acting on our shared values. One of our values is respect for all people. Over the last three years we've hired several highly qualified employees who have disabilities. Now we're creating a companywide training plan and I've been asked to lead the training effort. I'm concerned about meeting the needs of our employees with disabilities. What suggestions do you have?

Determined in Denver

Dear Determined:

WOW! You work for a great company and from your letter I can tell that you live your organization's values. That's a powerful combination. It's wonderful that you're thinking about these issues before the fact rather than waiting until the day of the training session. I'm certainly not an expert on this topic, but I have a few ideas and a possible resource.

There are four areas that come to my mind, and there are probably more, for you to consider.

Will people be able to see me, my visuals, or each other?

Will people be able to hear me or each other?

Will people be able to get to the training areas, break rooms, rest rooms, or other places we might go?

Will people be able to participate comfortably and fully in the activities I've planned?

Review your training session, as it currently stands, with these questions in mind. Every time you come to a section where you can't answer yes to all four of the questions, you need to come up with a plan B. If I were you, my next step would be to meet with some of your employees with various disabilities, ask for their help in finding answers, and do a reality check to see if you missed any questions. The people closest to an issue are most often the best people to offer a solution.

Other great resources are the associations that represent members with specific disabilities. Some may be local, others may be national, but all of them can be gold mines of information.

Some of the solutions to these issues may come with a price tag (interpreters, for example), but with your company's attitude, I don't think that will be too much of a problem. Some of the issues will simply require a little creativity. I'm convinced that all of the issues can be solved. Keep me posted on how everything works out. I'm anxious to hear.

Chris

Dear Determined:

It's great to hear from someone who is interested in meeting the needs of all participants. Here are my suggestions.

As you work to make sure everyone can see your visuals, remember that this may require a larger point size for the type you commonly use for slides, overhead transparencies, or flip charts. You might want to check into local resources for creating workbooks with large type.

Of course, not all disabilities are obvious. In one of my training sessions a participant complained about the types of chairs we were using and that she would suffer from a migraine if she didn't get something different to sit in. Not realizing the severity of her condition (I found out later she has crippling arthritis), and the fact that we were holding the training on site in her building, I suggested she check in one of the nearby offices. A few days later I received a letter from her, complaining to the training officer that my lack of sensitivity to her needs caused a migraine, and she lost two days of work as a result. This helped me realize that not all special needs are visible.

Several times in my training life, I have had Little People (dwarfs) in attendance, and two people in particular were grateful for a substitute footrest. On two different occasions I loaned out my handy trainer's case so these individuals could place their feet on it. They sat in regular chairs like everyone else, but of course, their feet couldn't reach the floor.

When working with interpreters I've always spoken to them first, and placed them in the front of the room there they could be comfortable. Most of the time I have had a pair working in shifts, as signing can be extremely fatiguing. I try to slow down my rate of speech ever so slightly when an interpreter is in the room.

If people using a wheelchair or crutches are attending my session I like to be sensitive to their limited mobility. If I count people off into groups, I arrange it so the people with disabilities can stay at their current table.

I've discovered that it can be difficult for a person with cerebral palsy or other mobility-limiting conditions to pull stickers off a paper backing (I have a couple of exercises in which people write a word onto a sticker and then give it away). If I know someone will have difficulties with this, I'll find an alternative activity.

I tend to avoid telling people to stand up and have a chat if someone is in a wheelchair, but I do still use visual words if I have a visually impaired person in my group. It pays to take a good look at your group and quickly determine what their needs might be. Most individuals with disabilities appreciate someone's asking, "Could you use some assistance with that door/chair/crossing the street?" before making a move to help them.

Again, because not all disabilities are observable, we need to have an extra ear or eye out for that exception.

Leslie

Dear Instant Trainers:

I work for a large dairy foods company that is in the midst of a massive system update. We've just purchased computers for all of our sales reps and I will be part of the new training team.

Our company has several locations, some in urban areas and some more rural, and in the past few years as our company has grown, our workforce has become more diverse. We want to reflect that in our sessions. We've been hearing a lot about diversity in the workplace, and would appreciate a crash course on the basics just so we're prepared to meet the needs of all of our sales reps, whoever they are and wherever they are. Is there anything our training team needs to know about communicating with a diverse group of professionals?

Sensitive in St. Paul

Dear Sensitive:

Your sales reps probably do represent a cross section of our society and it's an excellent policy to reflect their diversity in your language, audio-visual materials, and program content. Many voices have been raised in the last few years regarding diversity and the issue of political correctness is fresh in everyone's minds. Diversity awareness is simply common courtesy and you'll find it is quite effortless to employ respectful, inclusive language. Here are a few tips you and your teammates might find helpful:

- Make sure your audiovisual materials are representative of the people in your workplace. The most obvious factors are gender, age, ethnicity, and special needs or disabilities. Before you purchase clip art, check out the samples to determine whether it will offer you the diverse mix you want. I would say that most of today's presentation software packages are quite good and I have been impressed that even cartoons (those produced by the Click Art company, for example) feature a variety of men, women, ages, and races.

- Monitor your language to determine the level of bias in your orientation: Many people are (rightfully) offended by sexist language, so you'll want to ensure that you use both male and female pronouns and inclusive examples. This simply means you will say "he *and* she" either combined or alternatively rather than always using the pronoun "he."

- Using the "he and she" pronouns can be laborious. There's a simple solution: Make your word plural. For example, instead of saying, "In assessing each sales rep's needs, we've kept in mind that *he or she* will need to ..." try this approach: "In assessing the needs of all our sales reps, we've kept in mind that *they* will need to...."

- Use parallel references—"women and men," rather than "men and ladies" or "girls and men"—to avoid subtle undertones of inequality.

- Honor multicultural heritage and individuality. Avoid singling out superfluous details such as the color of a person's skin, origin of culture, gender, size, or age unless it is essential information. You'll find that most references are unnecessary. Examples: "This *woman* doctor …," "This *black* company president …," "This *Asian* manager …," "This *heavy-set* person…."

- If you use examples that criticize a particular behavior or work practice, make sure you don't always pick on a particular segment of the workforce. That is, avoid consistently making a woman (or white male, or member of a cultural, racial, sexual orientation, or disabled group) the culprit. In short, avoid any kind of diminution of individuals in any particular group.

- Avoid ageist inferences. Just as you want to avoid gender- or culturally-biased language, remember that references such as "little old man" or "little old lady" rob older people of their individuality and dignity.

- Avoid negative references to sexual orientation, too. Gay bashing, even when intended as humor, is in extremely poor taste and completely needless. You stand to lose more than anyone else by engaging in it.

- Maintain an open mind and you will open the minds of your learners. The major benefit of following the above guidelines is that, when you avoid the pitfalls of exclusionary language or references, you stay focused on your material!

These are just a few examples and obviously there is much more to the topic of workplace diversity. Perhaps these suggestions will help you avoid needlessly offending someone. Many of us have raised our awareness of these issues in the past few years and we are offended by words and references that were commonplace just a few years ago.

Generally, today we are less tolerant of intolerance. If you are interested in pursuing this topic further, consult *The Instant Trainer's* annotated bibliography (Appendix D).

A little bit of work on your part will not only increase your sensitivity to this topic, but will also address the sensitivities of your learners.

Leslie

Dear Sensitive:

When it comes to diversity, I'm one for common sense. Try this experiment. Think of the one thing that makes you the most different from the people you work with on a daily basis. It could be your age, baldness, color, gender, or a host of other things. Now imagine how it would feel if in every conversation, during every meeting, included in every introduction, this difference was highlighted. Or if in all the organization's publications, advertisements, and promotional material that highlighted employees or people using your products or services, there was never anyone who looked like you. Get the feeling?

Very few people in today's workplace are deliberately mean or cruel (and if they are, they don't deserve a job with your organization). However, lapses in judgment do occur. Your job as a role model is to work as hard as you can to eliminate those lapses. Thanks for caring!

Chris

 Dear Instant Trainers:

For the past four years I have worked as a Personnel Assistant in a large food service company and I must confess we haven't always kept up with the times. But it's a new dawn and we're waking up to the fact that there are ways of saying things that can either tune people into your message or tune them out. Because our customer base is so diverse, we recognize the need to update our language, both within our company and without. I have been assigned to teach what I would call a crash course on diversity, particularly in the area of gender-neutral references. I am wondering if you could help me out with a few tips on how to teach my group a few diversity skills. Any ideas?

Wordless in Waukegan

Dear Wordless:

Yes, there are a few that come to mind, and thank you for asking. With today's diverse workforce comes the need to pay attention to what we say and the spirit in which we say it. Those in the know are usually impressed when they recognize those who make an honest effort to include rather than exclude, and to show respect for others.

Exclusive male pronouns can become tedious to an educated audience:

"When a manager prepares for an appraisal, he wants to…"

"A good doctor knows he needs to…"

Assigning only female pronouns to a profession is another exclusionary practice:

"An effective secretary knows that she must always…"

"A surgical nurse builds her skills in…"

Avoid inappropriate (though well-intended) requests that slot or stereotype:

"Why don't you give us the woman's point of view…"

"Please give us the white male's perspective on that issue…"

Don't engage in bashing, bad-mouthing, or belittling any individual or representative group:

"Well, what did you expect from a man?"

"Trust a woman to say a thing like that!"

Avoid assuming that all members of a particular group are the same or that everyone wants the same kind of treatment. It helps to stop and consider how ludicrous it is to solicit a global opinion from *one* individual, as the above examples point out. Each of us can only speak from our own experience: Imagine the responsibility you'd feel if you were asked to speak for all of the women or men in your company, or for all new male or female trainers!

Diversity awareness simply means maintaining sensitivity about the differences and similarities between all of us, and honoring what sets us apart and what we have in common. If you create a respectful, learning-focused environment, you will find your trainees feeling more connected to you and to each other, and more willing and able to focus on why everyone is there: to learn.

Leslie

Dear Wordless:

Most of this book is about do-it-yourself solutions to problems and concerns. This is one area where you might consider getting some outside, profes-

sional help. If you contact the national office of ASTD (the address and phone number is in Appendix C) they will send you a Trainers and Consultant's Guide. I'm sure you'll find several highly qualified diversity training specialists in your area, who could either deliver a program for you or help you develop a meaningful and successful program for your team. Unfortunately, I've seen too many situations where in an attempt to save money, untrained, yet well-meaning, people have done more harm than good in organizations as they try to "do diversity."

Chris

DISCOVERING THE NEXT STEPS

We hope it's been fun for you!

We've loved writing this book. Spending time together, answering your questions about a subject we care deeply about, has been a rare treat. But this isn't the end.

Our last three questions reminded us of something important. Learning about how people learn, sharpening your training skills, or looking for new, creative ways to approach an old problem are the subjects of a course that never ends! For most of us, that's why training has such appeal—there's always something new to learn. School is never out for an Instant Trainer.

Maybe it's the enthusiasm for learning that makes a trainer great. Think back to those trainers and teachers who have made a difference in your life. What did they have in common? They had a passion for their subject and couldn't wait to share it with others. They were students of their field and were always adding new material to their classes. They had the mind-sets of learners and curiosity could have been any of their middle names. They were great listeners and seemed to hang on your every word. They got as excited as you did (sometimes even more) when you mastered a skill or idea, and actively celebrated your success.

How about you—would you qualify? Read this last chapter and look for a few more ideas that will extend your Instant Trainer experience beyond the final pages of this book!

 Dear Instant Trainers:

You've got to help me! I work in a large industrial manufacturing company and am a very, very junior member of the marketing department. When my boss first asked me to do a little training, I was flattered and said yes right away. I liked doing it and I guess I did a good job, because now doing the Orientation to Marketing class for people in other departments seems to be a part of my regular job. Here's my problem: I don't have enough time! How can I continue to do the kind of job I want to do as a trainer and keep up with my regular work in a way that will allow me to get ahead in the organization? Please make your answer short; I don't have enough time to read a long answer.

Fatigued in Fox Point

Dear Fatigued:

Okay, you asked for it short and to the point! Create a training system.

I suppose you want a little more than that. Instead of thinking about a training session, get in the habit of thinking about training units. Break your agenda into its parts: a lecture bit, a small group discussion, an activity, etc. Create a short checklist for each part—material covered, instructions detailed, equipment needed, etc., and each time you do your session, evaluate each part, not the entire session. The parts that go well, that give the learners what they need, and that fit your timing are okay as is and when you're ready to do the next session you can prepare by running through your checklists. The parts that don't fare as well, that need some more work on timing or techniques or maybe need to be replaced, are the ones you'll focus on next time.

Investing time in this process will, in the long run, allow you to build a repertoire of successful training components that will save you time in the future.

(Do you have a minute for two more sentences?) The ability to present ideas effectively is a career-builder in any profession. The extra time you invest in preparing training sessions for others is really an investment in yourself!

Chris

Dear Fatigued:

A few years ago one of my clients whose budget ran aground asked me to create a leader's guide and sell them my program. It sounded like a great idea but I didn't know where to begin. After weeks of procrastinating and panicking, I realized I had to get organized. The first thing I did was to break my program into time units—morning, afternoon, the first half of the morning, the second half, and so on. I kept crunching time into smaller and smaller units and all of a sudden the program fell into place. The clients still use the manual from time to time, and I gained a great lesson from the experience.

Leslie

Dear Instant Trainers:

I started out using your book as a quick reference. Then one day I sat down and read it from cover to cover. I've really enjoyed your humor and good practical advice. I'm also enjoying the training I'm doing and would like to do more. What else can I do to enhance my training skills?

Groupie in Grand Forks

Dear Groupie:

We both can remember feeling just like you several years ago. The most important thing a trainer can come to understand is that you are, in fact, a learner. If you want to continue to enhance your training skills, keep learning. Go to Appendix D, pick out a few of the books mentioned, and read them. Go to training sessions yourself and remind yourself what it feels like to be a learner. Join your local American Society for Training and Development (ASTD) chapter and attend their meetings. (The national address is in Appendix C.) Find a trainer buddy and agree to meet once a month for lunch to talk about your training triumphs and challenges. Take a class on a subject totally unrelated to your work and stretch yourself. Subscribe to *Training Magazine* or Bob Pike's *Creative Training Techniques Newsletter.* Look back at the end of each week and identify how you learned over the last seven days. Keep the spirit of learning alive in your heart. Your participants will thank you for it!

Chris

Dear Groupie:

Here's something you might be interested in trying; I've found it to be a great learning device as well as a great way to catalog new stories, fresh material, and good examples. Two years ago I began keeping a Trainer's Journal. *After a program, I write down my immediate reflections. Sometimes I record how I felt before, during, or after the session. Sometimes I describe special experiences, funny or touching things people tell me. It's given me a great record of my growth and development as a trainer and speaker. I wish I'd begun this practice two decades ago; I think it might have shortened my learning curve.*

Now, this approach may not work for you; keeping a journal isn't for everyone (Chris would attest to this!). But it is a great way of measuring your confidence and capabilities as a trainer. You're creative enough that you might not exactly create a Trainer's Journal, but you might come up with an equally effective approach for you!

Leslie

 Dear Instant Trainers:

I've searched your book from cover to cover and have found some helpful ideas, but **you didn't answer my question**!

Panicked in Pittsburgh

Dear Panicked:

Don't worry, help is as close as an E-mail message. If you send us a question at InsTrainer@aol.com, we'll be happy to respond. We suspect that yours isn't the only question we've missed, and we're hoping others will write us as well. Who knows, your question and our answer might just appear in the next edition of *The Instant Trainer*!

Chris and Leslie

Appendixes

TRAINING TOOLS YOU CAN USE!

EIGHT INSTANT CHECKLISTS

Checklist One: A Checklist for Keeping You Centered and Targeted

Before the Program:

__ Do I know what I want to cover; my key points?

__ Have I selected learning activities to reflect my objectives?

__ Am I using all available resources?

__ Have I selected appropriate materials and time frames?

__ Have all of the physical details been taken care of?

Getting Started:

__ Do I need a warm-up activity? If so, which one?

__ Am I clear on the desired outcome I want to create?

__ Is there anything that might hamper my relationship with the group? If so, how can I deal with it so it doesn't stand in our way?

__ Have I given a clear picture of what my learners can expect and when?

Staying on Target:

__ Have I planned physical activity or movement every hour?

__ Do I have an activity planned if we meet after lunch?

__ Have I provided a clear agenda to keep us on track?

__ Do my support materials help keep attention?

__ Have I encouraged/allowed enough group involvement?

__ Are we where we should be at a specified time?

Staying in Touch with the Group:

__ Am I closely observing body language?

__ Have I used enough repetition, examples, and illustrations?

__ Have I elicited enough group input to correctly read their reactions to this program?

__ Has there been enough participation / interaction?

__ Have I varied the format enough to control fatigue?

__ Have I reinforced major points with support materials?

__ Have I asked enough questions to adequately test their comprehension of what we've covered?

__ If I have noted fatigue, confusion, frustration, or resistance, have I responded to it?

__ Am I moving at a pace appropriate for this group?

__ Am I using the most effective approach for this group?

__ Am I being responsive to expressed needs or concerns?

Wrapping Things Up:

__ Have I summarized and answered all last questions?

__ Have I checked their comprehension of the material?

__ Have I left them with a feeling of closure?

__ Have I offered out-of-class options (books, tapes, resources, videos, other learning programs, etc.) for further study?

__ Have I been willing to hear private concerns, one on one?

__ Am I the last person to leave when the session is over?

Checklist Two: A Checklist to Monitor the Four Essential Factors in Training

Physical Factors

__ The room temperature is within comfort range to slightly cool.

__ There is adequate lighting and ventilation.

__ The size of the room and seating arrangement fit size of group.

__ Comfortable chairs are provided for participants.

__ Breaks and format variety are planned to offset fatigue.

Participant Factors

__ Group members share some level of acquaintance.

__ People know what to expect and what is expected of them.

__ They are invited to participate and feel safe to get involved.

__ Participants are positively reinforced for their contributions.

Content Factors

__ The material is relevant and designed for the group.

__ Material is reinforced through a variety of methods.

__ Participants are given adequate time to absorb material, ask questions, make contributions, and get actively involved.

Trainer Factors

__ The trainer establishes an immediate "presence."

__ Expectations are clearly stated ("We will …," or "I invite your participation.").

__ The trainer shares the responsibility for learning.

__ The trainer communicates with tact and respect for the learners, displaying a positive attitude toward the experience of learning.

__ The trainer controls time while balancing content and process.

__ The trainer invites and accepts feedback.

Checklist Three: A Sample Preprogram Questionnaire

Preparing for a training session should include time considering the participants as well as the time you spend on the course content. A questionnaire will help you get additional information about the organization/company/ department and the participants. Listed below are questions you may want to ask.

Group _____ Date _____

Participants

How many people will attend? _____ Percentage male? _____ Percentage female? _____

What is the average age of attendees? _____ What are their job responsibilities? _____

_____

How well will the participants know each other? _____

_____

Where is the session in the workday? _____ Beginning ___ Break ___ End of shift ___

Content

What is the reason for this training? _____

_____

How will people use the skills/knowledge learned during this training in their jobs? _____

_____

How will the skills/knowledge learned during this training be reinforced on the job? _____

_____

Are there concerns about this training that I should be aware of? _____

_____

What are employees' attitudes about this subject? _____

_____

Logistics

What type of room will I be working in? _____

Does the room size fit the group size? _____

Will quality of sound be an issue? _____

When can I get in to set up? _____

Checklist Four: Training Techniques

(We suggest using at least 4 to 5 different techniques in every session, to keep things lively.)

__ ICEBREAKER
A quick way to help everyone get acquainted; establishes a precedent for participation and discussion; establishes rapport; sets positive expectations.

__ LECTURE
Shares a lot of information in a brief period; builds a foundation for later application; defines and outlines key concepts.

__ HANDOUTS; PRINTED MATERIALS
Reinforce lecture and discussion; help pace the program; extend learning beyond the classroom.

__ QUESTION AND ANSWER
Clarifies and amplifies lecture material; encourages participation; allows learners to be self-directed; stimulates thinking.

__ GROUP DISCUSSION
Uses the learner as a resource; lets participants get acquainted; develops a sense of group identity; elicits questions.

__ GROUP PROBLEM SOLVING
Lets learners utilize what they know; establishes a sense of purpose; builds a team atmosphere; creates an emotional investment in the outcome they create.

__PAIRED DISCUSSION
Uses the learner as a resource; builds trust between participants; allows for more disclosure and individual involvement; great when time is limited.

__ WARM-UPS
Quick to facilitate; fun and lighthearted; prepare learners for involvement in a specific learning activity; often point out the need for learning the subject matter.

___ SELF-REPORT INSTRUMENTS

Let the learner self-evaluate privately; build self-assessment and self-monitoring skills; offer a referral tool for checking progress.

___ CASE STUDIES

Give participants a chance for in-depth exploration; offer practical application of a concept; encourage problem solving.

___ ROLE PLAYING

Offers a safe environment for learning new skills; places most group members at an even level; forces participants to practice the concepts and techniques presented.

___ DEMONSTRATION

Shows and tells; lays the foundation for skill development; uses sensory channels; generates questions; presents an overview.

___ ENERGIZERS

Offer a brief diversion; create a physical relief valve; rejuvenators for the body and mind; great for recharging the group's energy level.

___ REPORT OUTS

Give discussion groups a task focus and sense of closure; those selected as spokespersons have a leadership opportunity; lets everyone know what happened in each group.

___ RECORDED REPORT OUTS

Recorded information on a flip chart sheet or overhead can be used as a resource; participants have a chance to create a "product"; everyone learns from everyone.

___ SIMULATIONS

Offer participants a chance to generalize personal behavior toward real-life situations; encourage individual involvement.

___ CLOSURE ACTIVITY

Summarizes and sets the stage for action; sets expectations for on-the-job application; facilitates the transfer process; makes learners responsible for using what they've learned.

Four questions to help you decide which training techniques to use:

__ Who is your audience?

__ What is your purpose?

__ How much time do you have?

__ Which approach will best meet your needs?

Checklist Five: A Checklist for Staying on Schedule

__ Have you outlined time frames? Have you coordinated your watch with everyone else's?

__ Is the break length realistic for the facility (for example: slow elevators, other groups breaking at the same time)?

__ Have you openly discussed any lateness with the group?

__ Have you made a public statement about your expectations?

__ Have you personally invited people back into the room when breaks end?

__ Have you begun on time regardless of the number present?

__ Have you set up any kind of reward for returning on time?

__ Have you promised to give everyone a critical bit of information as soon as they return from break?

__ Can you begin your session with a small group discussion to allow for a few moments of grace for latecomers?

__ Have you announced not only the length of the break but also the actual "clock time" they are expected to return?

Checklist Six: A Checklist for Diagnosing the Causes of Low Participation

___ Is attendance voluntary or forced?

___ Has the format been varied, or could they be fatigued?

___ Are there any signs of peer pressure or subgroups?

___ Are you giving participants an opportunity to contribute?

___ Is one participant intimidating or influencing the rest of the group?

___ Is the temperature unusually cold or warm?

___ Was there a significant level of disclosure earlier and are they now withdrawing because it was a threatening experience?

___ Are they unclear of what's expected of them?

___ Is it time for a discussion?

___ Are you explaining your points too conceptually or abstractly and do you need to be more concrete?

___ Are you operating above their comprehension level?

Checklist Seven: A Checklist for Handling Difficult People and Situations

___ What is behind this person's resistance, hostility, or indifference?

___ What is this individual needing right now and how can I help?

___ What is the group needing right now and how can I help?

___ How can I best neutralize or energize this situation?

___ How can I control the training atmosphere without stifling?

___ How can I keep my ego out of this situation?

___ How can I remain focused on the problem rather than the person?

___ What preventive measures can I take to avoid potential pitfalls?

___ If it's too late for preventive measures, what can I do for damage control or to regain control in a non-controlling way?

Checklist Eight: A Checklist to Help You Identify Your Training Purpose

__ INFORMATION TRANSFER

Purpose: To inform the learner. You want participants to gain knowledge about a subject, concept, procedure, or principle.

Example: Orientation sessions and program updates.

Format: Content based. Lecture; question and answer.

__ AWARENESS

Purpose: To inform the learner. You want to get people's attention or raise their awareness about an issue, topic, or concern.

Example: Health maintenance or work safety.

Format: Content based. Lecture; question and answer; self-report instruments.

__ SKILL BUILDING/SKILL TRAINING

Purpose: To teach a task or specific technique. You want learners to develop specific, observable oral, written, or physical skills.

Example: Job Search and Interviewing.

Format: Role playing, hands-on, briefing, demonstration, and drill.

__ PROFESSIONAL DEVELOPMENT

Purpose: To increase the learner's general knowledge as it relates to nontechnical aspects of his or her job.

Example: Train the Trainer, Management Skills, Communication.

Format: Combination of lecture and discussion, group activities. May or may not include role playing for skill development.

TEN SUREFIRE WAYS TO GET AUDIENCE PARTICIPATION

#1 Know Your Audience and Address Their Personal Concerns

When you introduce a training session you want to set the tone for a positive, participative environment. Here is a practical and perceptive way of starting out on a positive note. While you may not actually be able to spend a good deal of time on each of these five areas, understanding these five key points will help you help your learners to relax and settle in as you begin.

Keep in mind that whenever people are asked (or told) they'll be attending some kind of training seminar or educational session, they come to the experience with some questions or reservations. How you open up your session can address their concerns and help put everyone at ease (this includes you, too). As you kick off your sessions, keep in mind that at some point in your program, each individual will be:

Expecting

Reflecting

Objecting

Connecting

Perfecting

If you are willing to take time to consider each of these five factors and how they affect a learning environment, you'll find your programs getting off the ground almost effortlessly. Let's briefly examine these five factors, one at a time.

- **Expecting**—Many of us come to a meeting with some level of anxiety, wondering if it will be worth our time, what the experience will be like, how we will be treated, and if we'll be asked (or forced) to participate. We wonder what will happen and when, and if it will be a positive or negative experience. You can reduce anxiety and uncertainty by laying out an agenda, outlining what group members can expect to learn, demonstrating how they'll be treated when they participate, and giving everyone a chance to get acquainted with your philosophy and style before you ask anything of them. Set positive expectations by expressing a sincere desire to help people learn and let them appreciate your sense of humor.

- **Reflecting**—Adult learning theory tells us that people relate best to practicality, relevancy, and personal application. They also need occasional opportunities to "go inside themselves" to think, review, and process information and determine how the content or activities relate to their situation. You can facilitate this process by giving your learners occasional opportunities to enjoy some "mental space." Just stop talking and explain you want to give everyone time to think, reflect, and consider what's been covered. They can review their notes, talk to each other, ask questions, or just sit for a moment and ruminate over what they've learned. You can end this short period of reflection with a Q & A session to fill in any loose ends. You'll be amazed at what a difference this makes!

- **Objecting**—Let's face it, some people consider a training session or seminar an inconvenience. They consider it an interruption rather than an opportunity, and they may come in with a negative attitude. You might witness resistance or apathy. Sometimes people resist information because they fail to see the relevancy, need time to digest it, have a personal agenda, or object to what they think you are going to do. If they come in with a negative attitude, they won't learn anything until their concerns have been addressed. This means that if you expect criticism about a particular issue or activity, you must acknowledge it early on, without excessive apology. This approach is often used in negotiations, when the other party's objections are raised even before he or she has a chance to complain or criticize. Using a third-party reference can also reduce potential defensiveness. You can say something like "Some of our team members initially thought we were going to _____, but ..." and then explain. If you think someone might question a learning activity (such as our ways of picking partners, item 9 in this appendix), offer a quick explanation: "At first, this might seem a little off base, but bear with me ..." How can anyone object if you bring it up first?

- **Connecting**—This is the "Aha!" of learning. It's that miraculous moment when an individual (or the entire group) gets a significant insight, revelation, or connection. These are the turns of mind, the paradigm shifts that take us to new levels of thinking; they are the whole reason trainers teach, instruct, and preach. You can further this purpose by encouraging participants to test, explore, and problem solve. Ask them to refine and redefine their ideas. By playing off what they already know and asking good questions (as in the debriefing model, SAGE, in this Appendix), let them make the discoveries. Let them tell you rather than you telling them. When people are free to make their own discoveries, their learning sticks!

- **Perfecting**—If you pay attention to what goes on in your classroom, you will learn a good deal from your learners. You'll witness participants taking your ideas and making them better. It's an exciting moment to see them fly with an idea and you'll know you've done your job when this happens. As you know, group outcomes are often superior to the efforts of one person. This is yet another example of learning from each other. We're all learners, even the trainers, and we can all keep trying to perfect what we do. Just think how *you* can perfect these five steps!

#2 Have Your Audience Practice the Skills You're Teaching Them

Practice is critical to success: If people don't try their new skills in your classroom where it's safe and structured, chances are they will never make the attempt back in the real world. However, many people are afraid they'll look foolish if they practice new skills in front of others, so you may need to encourage your trainees, and create a nonthreatening environment for them—where it's okay to make mistakes!

Setting the Stage:

- Begin with general questions that highlight the need for continual practice and skill building in nearly any endeavor. Examples:
  "When have you had to reprimand an employee and you struggled for the right words ... ."
  "How many times have you had to approach your manager with bad news...."

- Explain the need for practicing and preparing for such situations and the benefits of planning ahead. Let them know this is such an opportunity.

- Exhibit positive anticipation. Let your voice and body language communicate a sense of confidence that everyone is interested in skill practice and ready to go to work. If you seem tentative, they will, too. Boldly go where few trainers dare to go, into the world of role playing. Skill practice is the secret to skill building.

- Explain clearly what you intend to have happen, and that you expect everyone to participate. Describe and write down all instructions so participants can refer to them as needed.

- Use verbs that set up positive anticipation and results, such as:
  develop
  establish
  increase
  enhance
  create
  manage
  augment
  achieve
  integrate
  finesse

- Explain time frames, parameters, and expectations of results.

- Provide testimonials and results. Explain your own positive outcomes through skill practice. Invoke learning theory and any other metaphor or example you need to make your point.

Facilitating Skill Practice:

- Be available; let people know you'll be walking around and observing them; if they know this ahead of time they'll be more open when you walk up to them. Instruct them to continue their skill practice as you pass by (people have a tendency to stop whatever they're doing when the trainer approaches).

- Predict and "sell" the results of skill practice; let your group know what to expect by providing them with a predictive model. Say something like, *"You'll find in the beginning that this may seem a little artificial, and it is. But you'll also find that by attempting to simulate your real-life situation you'll become more comfortable using new words or approaches so you'll try it back on the job."*

- Encourage participants to use whatever resources they need—notes, references, reminders, or "cheat sheets"—to help them feel more comfortable or confident.

- Give people adequate time to privately practice and discuss the results. It helps if you keep track of time so you can lead them through the different steps.

- Be very clear on what they can expect and when. Repeat your instructions once or have them explain the process back to you to make sure they've got it.

#3 Round Robin Role Plays (Skill Practice)

The part about role playing that everyone hates is having to be alone, in front of the room, practicing a new skill while everyone is watching. Here's a different approach: a special structure designed for simultaneous, organized role playing (this means that everyone in the group will be engaged in role plays at the same time so no one feels singled out or pressured to perform). It really takes the pressure off!

Get participants into groups of three. To choose a method of succession for turn taking, each person will need to choose to be either an "A," "B," or "C," or you can assign them if you wish. As you have surmised, "A's" will go first, followed by "B's" with "C's" going last.

You need to plan your agenda so that there is enough time for each person in each triad to engage in skill practice. Most role plays tend to take between five and eight minutes depending on the complexity of the specific role play situation. Debriefing (discussing reactions to the role plays) may take even longer. For information on debriefing, check out the SAGE debriefing model elsewhere in this appendix.

Role plays need to fit the needs of your participants. If you are willing or able to custom design your material to fit your group, people can work on a role play you've designed ahead of time. Or, with a little bit of guidance from you they can create their own. (If you have not prepared the role plays in advance, review the Back Pocket Exercises in this Appendix so participants can take a few moments to create their own scenarios.)

There's a powerful aspect of conducting role plays with three rather than two people: The three roles rotate so everyone takes an active part in the skill practice. Each person will have an opportunity to be the Principal (the person practicing the new skill), the Respondent (other party), and the Observer.

For example, in your first role play, the "A's" will be the Principals, the "B's" the Respondents, and the "C's" the Observers. In the second role play, "B's" will be the Principals, "C's" will be the Respondents, and "A's" become the Observers. In your last and third round, "C's" will be the Principals, "A's" will be the Respondents, and "B's" will be the Observers. This equalizes the pressure: everyone gets to do everything, and in case you haven't guessed, much of the learning takes place when people are in the role of the Observer.

If you have prepared the role plays in advance, arrange it so that all of the "'A's" in the room will have the same role play to work with, as will all "B's" and "C's." You need to coordinate time lines so everyone starts and stops at the same time. While this may sound a bit confusing or labor intensive, you'll get the hang of it after a couple of run-throughs, and you'll be impressed with how smoothly this works.

Instructions for Monitoring the Process:

In keeping track of time for the group, let them know ahead of time how many minutes they will have for each round and carefully explain that each triad will first do Role Play #1, then #2, then #3. Instruct them to stop between each role play and wait for further instructions (this is worth repeating to ensure they really hear you). Allow time for debriefing time following each role play. You will want to monitor how long debriefing takes after each role play, considering you have three separate skill practices. Emphasize the importance of their following your time lines. You can write the flow of the "A - B - C" approach on a flip chart, board, or transparency (along with time lines) to use as a reference:

> Role Play #1—A is the Principal, B is the Respondent, C is the Observer
>
> Role Play #2—B is the Principal, C is the Respondent, A is the Observer
>
> Role Play #3—C is the Principal, A the Respondent and B the Observer

Time Projections:

Plan for about an hour to complete all three rounds of role plays. Be very clear to the group that you want them to *stop* after each role play and to wait for your instructions before moving on.

Approximate Time Frames:

Role Play: 5–8 minutes with prepared role plays. Participants need time to read it and prepare for it. If people create their own they will need time to explain it before they can begin practicing. With prepared role plays, the Principal and Respondent have each of their situations clearly outlined.

Debriefing in the triads: 3–5 minutes.*

Open Discussion in whole group: 5–15 minutes. (Experiment with this one. Try open group discussion after each role play and see how you like it. Next time, try it at the end of all three role plays and decide which you prefer).

*Triad Debriefing:

Ask the "A's" (the Principals) to talk about what they felt they did right and what was most difficult.

Ask the "B's" (the Respondents) their reactions to how the "A" behaved and if there was anything they wished the "A" had done or not done.

Ask the "C's" to give feedback to the "A", outlining what the "A" did right and offering constructive suggestions for future real-life situations similar to the role play. (The "B's" usually have the fewest comments to make but once in awhile they come up with something substantive.)

Disadvantages of This Method:

Takes a bit of time and energy to develop, organize, and orchestrate. If participants are using their own situations, you can plan on an extra 15 or 20 minutes. A visible matrix or flow chart helps so people can see how their roles will rotate. If you prepared role plays ahead of time, color code the sets so you can differentiate them.

Staple the A, B, and C sets in the proper order so the first page of the A's stapled set would show their role as Principals, the first page of the B's set would have their Respondents' role on top, and the C's first page would be that of the Observer, and so on. If you explain the instructions orally and write them down you ensure better success in moving from one role play to the other.

Advantages of This Method:

This approach equalizes the process for everyone. Each person takes an active role and no one is singled out. Even shy people tend to get involved because everything is all spelled out for them. The Observer role is a critical one, because this is where most of the learning takes place. The Observer can see and hear what is said and how the other party reacts to it. When the Observer gives feedback to the Principal, he or she heightens awareness of what happened and how it could be improved upon.

People appreciate not having to "go to the front of the room." The privacy of working with only three people reduces the amount of performance pressure.

Participants feel safe and more comfortable than if they had to role play in front of everyone, but if an issue comes up during debriefing, they are often willing to role play the situation in front of everyone else following the earlier role play because the private practice built up their confidence.

#4 Instant (Back Pocket) Activities

There may be times when your group gets tired, distracted, or listless—the perfect occasion for an instant group activity. We call these back pocket exercises because they can be conducted on the spot when they are most needed, with little preparation or supplies. They are so named because you can pull them out of your back pocket and instantly involve your learners.

Back Pocket Activity 1: Creating Instant Group Activities with Index Cards

Give every participant an index card (4 × 5 is the ideal size). Ask them to write down a problem or challenge they are currently experiencing at work and would appreciate some input on. Then choose any of the three options below.

Option 1.
Get people into pairs or groups of three and instruct them to take turns describing the situations they outlined on their index cards. Tell partners they are expected to ask questions and give suggestions, and encourage the speaker to write down any worthwhile or

workable solutions. This activity will take approximately 10 to 15 minutes for two people and up to 20 minutes for a threesome.

Option 2.

To save possible embarrassment and protect people's privacy, let them know ahead of time that they will be writing down a work situation that others will see and discuss. After participants have written down their situations on index cards as above (with enough detail to be easily understood by others), instruct them to throw their cards into a pile on a table. Everyone is then asked to pick up a card—not their own—and read the situation, and write down some analytical, exploratory questions, solutions, or suggestions that may help resolve the problem. You can repeat this process up to three times. Then lay out the cards out on a table, face up, and have each person locate his or her own. If you have extra time, you can let people explain their situations to the group and ask for more input if they wish. This is best done with large (5 × 8) index cards.

Option 3.

Assemble people into pairs and explain that they will have an opportunity to role play the situations they wrote on their cards. People will first explain them to their partners, and then they will practice the best way to handle them. This ensures customized role plays! If time allows, you can add a variation of Option 2 following the role play.

Back Pocket Activity 2: Instant Needs Assessment

It's helpful to understand what your learners expect from your training as well as what they bring to the training session. Here is a simple way to facilitate an icebreaker and conduct an instant needs assessment at the same time.

Pass out index cards and ask participants to divide their cards into four sections:

1. Why I am here or what I want to learn about this topic

2. My most difficult problem or challenge relating to this topic

3. One thing I already know about this topic

4. Skills I possess to help me deal with the challenges this topic presents to me

You can make up your own four central questions, too, depending on the point you wish to make. The specific information can vary, and the number of items you wish to cover can change, depending on the point you want to make or the specific topic you are covering.

Back Pocket Activity 3: On the Spot Answers

If you have a quiet or shy audience, or sense that participants may be reluctant to express what's really on their minds, give them index cards and have them write down their "burning" questions or concerns. Use the same color card for all participants so people won't feel singled out. Ask them to turn in their cards (face down if you sense there may be any sensitive issues).

Collect the cards, and organize them while the group is engaged in another activity. Then take a few moments to answer their questions or concerns in front of the whole group. This is a good way to warm up shy or reluctant audiences. It's also a great way to address people's specific concerns and it often generates in-depth discussion that might not otherwise take place.

Back Pocket Activity 4: Quick Mix

Before your session begins, create a series of three or four somewhat controversial statements relating to your topic (e.g., "The trainer is *fully* responsibility for the success or failure of a training session" or "Let's face it; some topics are boring by nature and not even the best trainer can do anything about it"). You probably get the sense that you want to create sweeping statements, yet there must be enough substance to create opposing views. With masking tape, post sheets of paper on the wall a small distance from each other, one at a time (flip chart paper is excellent for this purpose) with your statements written on them. Note: You could also use transparencies if you don't have a flip chart.

Using standard size sheets of paper (8 1/2 × 11), write the following. On one sheet, in large letters, write SA (which stands for strongly agree); on the next, place an A (agree); then a question mark or NS (not sure); write a D (disagree), and last, SD (strongly disagree) and tape all five of these sheets in strategic spots on the wall throughout the room. Make the letters large so people can see them and use a different color paper for each sign.

Read your first statement to the group once or twice and let them think about it. Ask your participants to silently reflect on their reactions and then instruct them to get up out of their seats and go stand near the sheet that most closely reflects their opinion. With any luck, there will be more than one person at each location. Let them talk in their small groups, then switch to open discussion.

Review the section on asking questions to help you formulate the kinds of questions that guarantee participation. Once you feel the energy for the discussion has dropped, immediately go on to your next statement. Or, if you are using this activity as an energizer or for variety in routine, save the next question for later. This back pocket activity makes for a nice break if people have been sitting for some time, and serves as a getting-acquainted exercise as well. Substantive discussions come out of this activity if you make sure the statements have enough "guts" so people's opinions will vary!

#5 SAGE: A Debriefing Model

Debriefing is the process of facilitating self-reflection and discovery. Skillful facilitators live and die by this process. You'll learn a good deal by developing your skills in conducting effective debriefings, and so will your participants. The secret is in asking good questions. Keep in mind that the best learning takes place when we teach ourselves. Debriefing is designed to facilitate self-discovery. You will find the following ideas both fun and fascinating.

After learning about the importance of making self-reflection a major part of seminars several years ago, Leslie created her own four-step debriefing model. We're delighted to share it with you. SAGE represents four simple steps to help you bring out the best in your learners so they can make their own critical connections and insights. Your ability to internalize and apply this model can make all the difference for your participants.

As you know, delivering the content isn't enough. Once the material has been presented, program participants need to take time to reflect on the process part of their learning experience. Following role plays, simulations, learning games, or problem-solving exercises, this debriefing model will help you expand on what everybody learned.

Let's cover a few philosophical and logistical points first:

- Please keep in mind that most of us know a good deal more than we think, and that a skillful trainer can bring out everyone's innate wisdom and best ideas.

- The longer the simulation or activity, the longer the debriefing should be for maximum effectiveness.

- The debriefing may take almost as long as the exercise or simulation itself.

- If you present the information strategically, most people can draw their own correct assumptions.

Following a simulation, learning game, role play, or structured activity, participants need to explore WHAT went on and HOW or WHY it went on. That's what SAGE can do for you!

S stands for SHARE.

The opening step is an exploratory phase characterized by a series of open-ended questions which ask that participants reflect upon and report their experiences. Whether they experienced a role play, simulation, game, or content based activity, the primary question you want answered is WHAT WENT ON? In the Share phase you ask participants to describe what they saw, felt, thought, or observed during the activity. You might ask questions such as:

- WHAT DID YOU SEE OR HEAR?
- WHAT WAS YOUR REACTION TO THAT?
- WHAT WERE YOUR EXPECTATIONS BEFORE YOU BEGAN?
- WHAT DID YOU THINK WHEN...?
- WHAT ELSE DID YOU OBSERVE?

The A stands for ANALYZE.

This is where the real reflection begins. In this phase, you ask participants for their interpretations of what they think happened. People are asked to analyze their experiences and draw personal conclusions as to cause and effect. The primary question centers around WHY people reacted as they did. Learners are asked to contrast, compare, infer, explore, and analyze not only what happened, but why. These kinds of questions will help you draw out people's perceptions and interpretations.

- WHY DO YOU THINK YOU (THEY) RESPONDED THAT WAY?
- WHY DO YOU THINK THAT HAPPENED IN THIS ACTIVITY?
- HOW DID THAT AFFECT (YOU) (THE GROUP)?
- WHY IS THIS KIND OF REACTION SIGNIFICANT?
- WHAT DOES (YOUR) (THE GROUP'S) REACTION SUGGEST?

G stands for GENERALIZE.

Once your group members have identified and analyzed what happened in their structured activity, you now want them to relate their experience to real life. This is the "transfer" phase where an insight gained will be transferred back into one's everyday existence. You will ask participants to connect what they just experienced with their world. The primary question is HOW, as in HOW DOES THIS RELATE TO REAL LIFE? You want people to recognize how their behavior in this simulation or exercise mirrors how they normally behave. By asking your learners to generalize in the classroom how their group experience relates to situations they face each day at work or at home, you have raised their awareness to a new level. Insight, realization, self-reflection, and personal analysis often result in permanent behavior or attitude change.

You can help people generalize and transfer information back to their world by asking questions such as:

- WHAT PRINCIPLES WERE OPERATING DURING THIS EXPERIENCE?
- WHAT KINDS OF CONCLUSIONS CAN YOU DRAW ABOUT (PEOPLE) (LIFE) (WORK TEAMS), etc. AS A RESULT?
- HOW DOES WHAT HAPPENED HERE RELATE TO WHAT HAPPENS TO YOU AT (WORK) (HOME)?

- WHEN HAVE YOU EXPERIENCED A SIMILAR SITUATION IN REAL LIFE AND WHAT WAS THE OUTCOME?
- WHAT DID YOU LEARN FROM THIS EXPERIENCE?

E stands for EVALUATE.

Once you've conducted this experience, asked your questions, facilitated the opportunity for insights and learning points, take a few moments to determine the effectiveness of this learning activity. The primary question is HOW WELL DID THIS WORK FOR YOU? Examine the simulation, role play, discussion, or case study for strengths, weaknesses, and suggestions that could improve the activity.

The evaluation phase is most critical the first two or three times you introduce a new learning activity so you can work the bugs out, and you will be amazed at the wonderful suggestions you'll receive from participants. Their input will help you get better and better! The kinds of questions you ask in the evaluation phase would include:

- WHAT KIND OF EXPERIENCE WAS THIS FOR YOU?
- WAS THIS AT ALL CLOSE TO REAL LIFE?
- HOW MIGHT IT HAVE BEEN MORE MEANINGFUL?
- IF YOU WERE TO EXPERIENCE THIS TYPE OF ACTIVITY AGAIN, WHAT KINDS OF CHANGES WOULD BE IN ORDER?

Once you have successfully run through an activity two or three times and it has run smoothly for you each time, you can eliminate the evaluate step. As one of our participants so aptly put it, at some point you don't have to SAGE; you can just SAG instead. Of course, you will always want to ask for and remain open to any suggestions for improvement.

Using the SAGE model can help you effectively debrief simple role plays and complex simulations. In the beginning, we suggest you write down your initial process questions (between four and six questions for each step) and additional questions will naturally follow. In time you'll internalize the steps of sharing, analyzing, and generalizing (and evaluating, when necessary or appropriate) and written questions will no longer be necessary. You'll also improve your facilitation skills along the way.

#6 Participation Strategies for Treating Physical Fatigue

Even the most enthusiastic learners can get tired, but you have many options in the prevention and/or treatment of physical fatigue.

1. Use questions to stimulate interest and hold attention. Hypothetical questions are nice: "You may be thinking …" or "Now, if you're wondering why …" as they ask for emotional involvement. Every now and then you can even include subtle statements about how the learner will benefit from a particular idea. This will keep participants focused on the relevancy of what you are saying and how it personally relates to them.

2. Offer periodic stretch breaks. Even one minute of mild physical activity can rejuvenate a group's collective energy level. Instruct people to stand up, give themselves room in which to move their arms freely and invite them to participate. Learn a few standard stretches or office yoga movements that can be done from either a standing or seated position (you can use the latter if you have anyone injured or disabled in your group).

3. Quick mixes are a good energizer: if you are at a point where people could discuss the material you have just been presenting, break them into discussion groups. To ensure that nearly everyone moves physically, number them off or assign them into groups. It's often best if you remain in charge of group formation. People tend to be nonassertive when fatigued and they will probably appreciate your instruction. Give them clear directions on what you want them to discuss in their groups.

4. If your group is large, time is limited, or there are other logistical constraints making a physical stretch break inconvenient, you can advise participants to stand up and engage in a discussion with one or two people near them. Be very clear that you want every-

one to stand up and remain standing during their discussion and reinforce your words nonverbally (motion with your arms that you want and expect them to stand up).

5. If you are not at a point where a discussion will work, or you have already used a stretch break, but if people have been seated in the same spot for more than an hour and you are sensing their fatigue, you can initiate "musical chairs" and simply ask everyone to change seats. (This is perfect if you are teaching change management.) (Of course, you do not want to use this method if space is limited and it is obviously inconvenient for people to change places. If you use this technique, use it no more than twice in a day.

6. You can ask people to speak to someone nearby in groups of two. If you need to cover more material before you can initiate a group discussion, if time is limited, or if physical movement would be inconvenient, simply ask participants to turn to one of the people closest to them and in pairs discuss their interpretation of what you've been saying. This can perk up the energy level of the group and may also trigger some questions and answers.

7. If you are sensing possible fatigue symptoms you can also directly ask the participants how they are feeling. "Are you feeling low in energy right now?" "Would you like to do some physical exercises that will help perk you up?" "Can you hang in there for another fifteen minutes?" It helps to do a perception check with your group so you can verify if what you are interpreting as fatigue is indeed that or if something else is going on.

8. Another fatigue fighting strategy is to give your group a five-minute break on the hour. This is, of course, in addition to your regular 10- or 15-minute break. You will find this 5-minute break time especially helpful when you are working a long training day. It keeps the energy level high and does not detract from the flow of the program.

#7 Using Questions to Encourage Learner Involvement

Here are three types of involving questions or statements you can use to help elicit comments, invite opinions, or encourage active participation:

- HYPOTHETICAL questions and statements gain attention and help draw the person into your presentation. Hypothetical questions don't always require an actual answer to the question but they involve participants emotionally and help them visualize a personal situation. Here are some examples:

  "How many times have you...?"

  "Think of how much time you would save if..."

  "If you've ever thought about how convenient it would be..."

  These questions don't presume a direct answer, but they do ask for mental involvement.

- ANTICIPATORY questions and statements build suspense. They ask participants to get involved and stay involved by building up to what is about to come. Anticipatory questions include:

  "You may be wondering..."

  "You're probably beginning to figure out that you could..."

  "Have you noticed a pattern here?"

  They stimulate your learners and keep them moving along with you.

- EXPLORATORY questions stimulate participants to tap into their personal experiences. They ask people to visualize or answer a question. Examples:

  "Have you ever wondered...?"

  "How many times have you asked yourself...?"

  "How many times have you been inconvenienced by...?"

These questions may or may not elicit direct responses, but they do get people emotionally involved.

- DIRECTIVE questions ask for an actual response. Use them when you want a testimonial or report of a real-life experience. Here are some examples:

  "Who in here has had the experience of…?"

  "Who would like to describe a situation where you have…?"

  "Who is willing to report an experience in…?"

You will see heads move, smiles of acknowledgement, and agreement or disagreement when you use involving questions. They are designed to get and maintain attention. Using these kinds of questions will help generate additional questions from participants, too.

Real learning takes place when people draw their own conclusions rather than having the trainer make the connections for them. Skillful use of questions and involving statements will help elicit the participant reaction you want: active learner involvement.

#8 Inviting Participation by Using People's Names

The more involved you get with your group, the more likely they'll get involved with you and your program. If you're an in-house trainer, maybe you will know everyone in your group. But if you don't know everyone, make it a point to learn people's names and use them.

Don't think you have to become some kind of memory expert. Using name badges, table cards, and some kind of structured introductions can help you get acquainted with your learners quickly. If you have the desire to truly know who is in your program and all about their personal situations, you'll find yourself remembering people and their names with ease.

Here are some ways of encouraging participation by using people's names:

- If a person puts only initials on the name badge or card, ask if that is how he or she would prefer to be addressed.

- Pronounce the name as the participant does and avoid diminutives without asking (check ahead of time whether Robert wants to be "Bob" or Debra, "Debbie"). If people introduce themselves with the more formal name, use it.

- Occasionally people will write one name on the badge or table card and call themselves a variation of that name. If you're ever uncertain about how a person wants to be addressed, ask.

You may be wondering how you can learn everyone's name if your group is large, but there are subtle ways. For example:

- If you are using tent cards, look down at people's cards as you walk around the room, catch their names, and repeat them to yourself while they are immersed in an activity. Systematically work your way around the room.

- Say a person's name while you are looking at him or her. People enjoy being singled out when it's a positive experience and there is nothing more expected of them than to simply be present. All they have to do is be there; they get instant credit for just showing up. And your stock goes up because you've taken the time to know your learners.

- In addition to names and faces, make an effort to remember people's stories. When people tell you about a situation they are currently facing (problem, challenge, victory, or whatever), remember it. If people make excellent comments (the kind worth repeating that perfectly illustrate a point you may be making), refer to what they said earlier. Of course, make sure it's a positive example so you can hold that individual up to the group rather than make a spectacle of them.

People love that you remember what they tell you. They feel like a real part of the process. Once you gain some experience as a trainer and build your confidence, you can "bond" yourself with the group by bringing them into the action more. You can intersperse people's names in your presentations if you know who they are. Most people enjoy hearing their names, and upon hearing them, their attention perks up.

#9 One Dozen Strategies for Picking Partners

It's nice to offer variety in whatever you do. Here are some ways to get people mixed up (at least physically!) without having to use the same old approach every time. You can suggest that your learners choose a partner by finding a person who has:

- matching dates on a penny
- the closest birthday to yours
- the same shoe size
- the closest matching length of hair
- the closest height
- the same sock or stocking color
- the closest number of paying jobs in a career
- the same type of watch face numbers
- the closest length of employment with the company
- the closest number of pieces of jewelry or buttons
- the same color jacket or shirt
- the closest amount of hair on their head
  Wait, let's make it a baker's dozen!:
- the same color or style of watchband

If these seem juvenile, they are. Choosing a partner always elicits that third-grade fear of "What if I don't get picked?" These techniques are designed to eliminate insecurity and level the playing field. Instead, people are thinking, "I can't believe we're doing this!" Oversee the process and if you have an odd-numbered group (not an odd group!) just make one of the pairs a triad.

#10 One Dozen Strategies for Putting Participants into Groups

Getting groups together can take time away from your training session and dampen the spirits of the group if people feel uncomfortable about finding their place. Here are some proven strategies to make group formation quick, easy, and fun. For each of these techniques, you'll need to determine ahead of time the number of groups you want to form so you have the correct number of props.

You can invite people to form groups by …

- matching the colored dots on their name badges
- matching the stickers (stars, lightening bolts, rainbows, suns, etc.) on their name badges
- distributing small wrapped candy pieces (Tootsie Rolls, Hershey's Kisses, Werther's Butterscotch, etc.) and having people find others with the same type of candy
- distributing playing cards and having them find people with cards of the same suit
- distributing cardboard shapes and having them find people with a matching shape
- giving people colored pipe cleaners and having them find people with the same colors
- distributing small toys (cars or animals) and having them find people with matching toys
- placing a colored paper clip on the handouts and having people look for the color matches
- using the old school standby—count off by the number of groups you want (1..2..3..4..5)
- distributing small pieces of paper with food items and having people find meal combinations (hamburger, fries, Coke, catsup, and mustard)

- giving participants colored pencils to write with and then having them form groups based on the colors of the pencils
- distributing small pieces of paper with lines from familiar songs and having people find others who have the lines that complete the song

Yet again, an Instant Trainers' bonus:

- using young children's floor puzzles with very large pieces and having people complete the puzzle to form a group.

Distributing is best done by putting the items in a paper bag (or bags if you have a larger group) and asking people to pick an item from the bag. This ensures a random distribution and avoids any sense of *rigging* the groups.

Some of these methods can be used more than once. For example, if you use the colored dots, the first group can be formed by all the same colored dots gathering into a group. A second group can be formed by having one of each color in the group. A third group can be formed by having another mixed color group but stating that no one can be in a group with someone they've been in a group with before.

Let your imagination go. Soon you'll have your own personal list of grouping strategies. Keep us posted on the ones that work the best!

THE BEST ELEVEN RESOURCES FOR TRAINERS

The association for trainers to join:

American Society for Training and Development

   1640 King Street

   Box 1143

   Alexandria, VA 22313-9833

   703-683-8100

   Membership includes a subscription to the *Training and Development Journal.* Call them for information about a local chapter in your area.

The books about training theory to have in your library:

   The Mager Six Pack by Robert F. Mager, Ph.D.

   Preparing Instructional Objectives

   Measuring Instructional Results

   Analyzing Performance Problems

   Goal Analysis

   Developing Attitude Toward Learning

   Making Instruction Work

   Each book is available separately. Complete reference is in Appendix D.

The books about training activities to have in your library:

   The Games Trainers Play Series by John W. Newstrom and Edward Scannell

   Games Trainers Play

   More Games Trainers Play

   Still More Games Trainers Play

   Even More Games Trainers Play

   Each book is available separately. Complete reference is in Appendix D.

The magazine to subscribe to:

Training Magazine

   50 South Ninth Street

   Minneapolis, MN 55402-9973

   612-333-0471

The newsletter to subcribe to:

Creative Training Techniques Newsletter from Bob Pike

Lakewood Publications
50 S. Ninth Street
Minneapolis, MN 55402
612-333-6526
oakwolf@wavefront.com email

The clip art provider to order a catalog from:

T/Maker Company

1390 Villa Street
Mountain View, CA 94041
800-986-2538
http://www.clickart.com

The catalog with fun and different training supplies:

Creative Learning Tools

P.O. Box 37
Wausau, WI 54402-0037
715-842-2467
715-848-9463 fax
CreativeLT@aol.com
Call them for information about the Instaframe.

Two catalogs for training publications:

McGraw-Hill

800-2 MCGRAW
614-759-3644 fax
http://mcgraw-hill.inforonics.com/cgi/listit?subjectkey=Training

Pfeiffer & Company

8517 Production Avenue
San Diego, CA 92121
619-578-5900
619-578-2042 fax
http://www.pfeiffer.com

The place for learning music:

OptimaLearning

Barzak Educational Institute International
885 Olive Ave.
Suite A
Novato, CA 94945-2455
800-672-1717

The place for fast and easy training program booklets:

Crisp Publications

1200 Hamilton Court
Menlo Park, CA 94025-1427
800-442-7477

The place for slides and overheads:

Genigraphics

In Focus Systems, Inc.
1689 Nonconnah Blvd.
Suite 118
Memphis, TN 38132
800-790-4001
800-790-4002 fax
http://www genigraphics.com

ENOUGH TITLES TO MAKE A BOOKAHOLIC TRAINER HAPPY FOR A VERY LONG TIME

General Training Books

Broad, Mary L. and John Newstrom. *Transfer of Training: Action-Packed Strategies to Ensure High Payoff from Training Investments.* Addison Wesley Longman, Boston, MA, 1992.
Training only counts when the techniques and ideas presented are applied. Broad and Newstrom share their considerable wisdom so you can enhance your training sessions.

Eitington, Julius E. *The Winning Trainer: Winning Ways to Involve People in Learning,* third edition. Gulf Publishing Company, Houston, TX, 1989.
No matter what kind of training you're doing, we'd bet that you'll find some great ideas for you. Eitington has put just about everything you'd ever want to know about training in one book. This book works like an entire library.

Jaques, David. *Learning in Groups,* second edition. Gulf Publishing Company, Houston, TX, 1991.
Based on the premise that learning happens better in groups than in lectures, this book provides a resource for group dynamics in a learning setting. You'll find lots of food for thought with practical information.

Kirkpatrick, Don. *Evaluating Training Programs: The Four Levels.* Berrett-Koehler Publishers, San Francisco, CA, 1994.
The book about evaluating training. If you want to learn ways to really measure the effectiveness of your training, this book will teach you how.

Knowles, Malcolm. *Self-Directed Learning,* fifth edition. Follett Publishing, Chicago, IL, 1975.
Don't let the copyright date put you off. Knowles' work is as applicable today as it was when originally written. If you want a brief but in-depth look at how adults learn and what they need as a result, this little volume will do it.

Mager, Roger F. *The Mager Six Pack.* Lake Publishing Company, Belmont, CA, 1984.

(Each book is available separately.)
Preparing Instructional Objectives

Measuring Instructional Results

Analyzing Performance Problems

Goal Analysis

Developing Attitude Toward Learning

Making Instruction Work

Another valuable resource for learning about how learners learn, how to make sure your training sessions work, and how to measure your efforts. If you work in a larger organization, ask around. Someone, somewhere in your organization has this set. It's a training classic.

Pike, Bob. *Creative Training Techniques Handbook: Tips, Tactics and How-To's for Delivering Effective Training,* second edition. Lakewood Publications, Minneapolis, MN, 1989.
Bob Pike's wisdom, gathered from his extensive experience as a master trainer, is gathered between the pages of this wonderful resource.

Race, Phil and Brenda Smith. *500 Tips for Trainers.* Gulf Publishing Company, Houston, TX, 1996.
An easy-to-read format makes this book a great resource for new and seasoned trainers.

Senge, Peter. *The Fifth Discipline: The Art and Practice of the Learning Organization.* Currency Doubleday Books, New York, NY, 1990.
This is the book that made the words *the learning organization* famous. Senge has a great impact on the way training is viewed and practiced in organizations. This book has the theory; the next book in our list has the tools for implementation.

Senge, Peter, Art Kleiner, Charlotte Roberts, Richard Ross, and Bryan Smith. *The Fifth Discipline Handbook: The Art and Practice of the Learning Organization.* Doubleday, New York, NY, 1994.
Consider this an essential for your library. Filled with concepts that support learning in a turbulent work environment, you'll also discover a wealth of exercises and activities you can conduct in your classroom.

Silberman, Mel. *Active Training: A Handbook of Techniques, Designs, Case Examples, and Tips.* Lexington Books, New York, NY, 1990.
This book is one of the most often used resources on our bookshelves, a great blend of theory and practical examples. A must-have for trainers who believe training is more than a lecture.

Williams, Linda Verlee. *Teaching for the Two-Sided Mind: A Guide to Right Brain/Left Brain Education,* third edition. Simon & Schuster, Inc., New York, NY, 1983.
This book is ostensibly for traditional teachers, but it has much to offer trainers, too. You'll find it is rich with exercises and activities that can help you understand how we learn. You'll discover ideas you can apply immediately, for yourself as well as your learners.

Training Activities Books

You don't have to think up an activity each time you need one. Here is a collection of books that have more exercises than you'll ever need. If you can only afford one, the Instant Trainers recommend one of the titles in the *Games Trainers Play* series.

Christopher, Elizabeth M. and Larry E. Smith. *Leadership Training: A Source Book of Activities.* Nichols Publishing Company, East Brunswick, NJ, 1993.

Engel, Herbert M. *Handbook of Creative Learning Exercises,* second edition. HRD Press, Inc., Amherst, MA, 1994.

Epstein, Robert. *Creativity Games for Trainers: A Handbook of Group Activities for Jump Starting Workplace Creativity.* McGraw-Hill, New York, NY, 1996.

Forbes-Greene, Sue, ed. *The Encyclopedia of Icebreakers: Structured Activities That Warm-up, Motivate, Challenge, Acquaint, and Energize.* Pfeiffer and Company, San Diego, CA, 1989.

Gordon, W., E. Nagel, S. Myers, and C. Barbato. *The Team Trainer: Winning Tools and Tactics for Successful Workouts.* Irwin Professional Publishing, Chicago, IL, 1996.

Hartzler, Meg and Jane E. Henry. *Team Fitness: A How-to Manual for Building a Winning Work Team.* ASQC Quality Press, Milwaukee, WI, 1994.

Jones, Ken. *Imaginative Events for Training: A Trainer's Sourcebook of Games, Simulations, and Role-Play Exercises.* McGraw-Hill, New York, NY, 1993.

Kroehnert, Gary. *100 Training Games.* McGraw-Hill, New York, NY, 1992.

Mill, Cyril R. *Activities for Trainers: 50 Useful Designs.* University Associates, San Diego, CA, 1980.

Newstrom, John, and Edward Scannell. *The Big Book of Business Games.* McGraw-Hill, New York, NY, 1996.

Nilson, Carolyn. *Games That Drive Change.* McGraw-Hill, New York, NY.

Nilson, Carolyn. *Team Games for Trainers: High-Involvement Games and Training Aids for Developing These and Other Team Skills.* McGraw-Hill, New York, NY.

Pfeiffer, J. William, ed. *The Encyclopedia of Group Activities: 150 Practical Designs for Successful Facilitating.* Pfeiffer and Company, San Diego, CA, 1989.

Rees, Fran. *25 Activities for Teams.* Pfeiffer and Company, San Diego, CA, 1993.

Scannell, Edward and John Newstrom. *Even More Games Trainers Play.* McGraw-Hill, New York, NY.

Scannell, Edward and John Newstrom. *Games Trainers Play.* McGraw-Hill, New York, NY, 1980.

Scannell, Edward and John Newstrom. *More Games Trainers Play.* McGraw-Hill, New York, NY, 1983.

Scannell, Edward and John Newstrom. *Still More Games Trainers Play.* McGraw-Hill, New York, NY, 1991

Silberman, Mel. *101 Ways to Make Training Active.* Pfeiffer and Company, San Diego, CA, 1995.

Snow, Harrison. *The Power of Team Building Using Ropes Courses.* Pfeiffer and Company, San Diego, CA, 1992.

Speciality Training Books

Some training subjects deserve books of their own. Here are some of the books on specific subjects that we've found helpful

Brandt, Richard C. *Flip Charts: How to Draw Them and How to Use Them.* Pfeiffer and Company, San Diego, CA, 1989.

Friedberger, Julie. *Office Yoga: Tackling Tension with Simple Stretches You Can Do at Your Desk.* Harper Collins Publishers, New York, NY, 1991.

Gredler, Margaret. *Designing and Evaluating Games and Simulations: A Process Approach.* Gulf Publishing Company, Houston, TX, 1994.

Jamieson, David and Julie O'Mara. *Managing Workforce 2000: Gaining the Diversity Advantage.* Jossey-Bass Publishers, San Francisco, CA, 1991.

Loomans, Diane and Karen Kolberg. *The Laughing Classroom: Everyone's Guide to Teaching with Humor and Play.* H J Kramer, Inc., Tiburon, CA, 1993.

Petit, Ann. *Secrets to Enliven Learning: How to Develop Extraordinary Self-Directed Training Materials.* Pfeiffer and Company, San Diego, CA, 1994.

Tulgan, Bruce. *Managing Generation X: How to Bring Out the Best in Young Talent.* Merritt Publishing, Santa Monica, CA, 1995.

Bonus Section—Creativity Enhancers

Here's our bonus book list. We don't think you can separate good training from creative thinking. Here are some of our favorite books on the subject of creativity. Enjoy!

Ayan, Jordon. *Aha!: Ten Ways to Free Your Creative Spirit and Find Your Great Ideas.* Crown Trade Paperbacks, New York, NY, 1997.

Michalko, Michael. *Thinkertoys: A Handbook of Business Creativity for the 90s.* Ten Speed Press, Berkeley, CA, 1991.

Rose, Colin. *Accelerated Learning.* Dell Trade Paperback, New York, NY, 1987.

Von Oech, Roger. *A Whack on the Side of the Head: How to Unlock Your Mind for Innovation.* Warner Books, New York, NY, 1983.

Wycoff, Joyce. *Mindmapping: Your Personal Guide to Exploring Creativity and Problem Solving.* Berkley Publishing Company, New York, NY, 1991.

Wycoff, Joyce and Tim Richardson. *Transformation Thinking: Tools and Techniques That Open the Door to Powerful New Thinking for Every Member of Your Organization.* Berkley Books, New York, NY, 1995.

Appendix E

TWO SAMPLE TRAINING EVALUATION FORMS

Evaluation Form 1

Session Title _____ Session Date _____

(All ratings are from the lowest 1 to the highest 5.)

I would rate the content of this session:

1.....2.....3.....4.....5

Because _____

I would rate the delivery of the content in this session:

1.....2.....3.....4.....5

Because _____

I would rate my participation during this session:

1.....2.....3.....4.....5

Because _____

The most important part of this session for me was... _____

_____

The part of this session I would change was... _____

_____

Thanks for your comments and suggestions!

Evaluation Form 2

Dear Participant:

On ___(Date)___ you attended my session on _____(Subject Matter)_____.
The real test of a training session happens when you return to the real world and try to use the techniques and apply the ideas you learned during the session. So I can make my session better the next time, I'd appreciate your feedback.

As a result of the training session, here's what I tried: _____

_____

_____

Here's how it worked: _____

_____

_____

Here's a question I have remaining about this subject: _____

_____

_____

If I went to another training session about this subject, here's something else I'd like to learn:

_____

_____

_____

Thanks for your input. I appreciate it!

INDEX